Praise for
Celebrate Customer Service

"What a great concept . . . service as a celebration! In order to sustain a quality environment, a new way of looking at service is required. Celebrating it is a perfect place to begin."
— Holly Stiel, *Ultimate Service*

"*Celebrate Customer Service* is a valuable resource for those who want to learn both the traditional and latest techniques in customer service."
— Michael LeBoeuf,
How to Win Customers and Keep Them for Life

"Truly great customer service affects every individual and every process at all levels of an organization. This book clarifies how to do this important job and what tools you will need."
— Keith Bailey and Karen Leland, *Customer Service for Dummies*

"How can you deliver great service day in, day out? *Celebrate Customer Service* is chock full of practical ways to give your customers what they want—great service that keeps them coming back again and again."
— Nancy Artz, PhD, *301 Great Customer Service Ideas*

"If you want to sell at higher prices, pay particular attention to this book—especially the part about the value of customer service."
— Lawrence L. Steinmetz, *How to Sell at Prices Higher than Your Competitors*

"I feel lucky if I get one good idea from a book. Read *Celebrate Customer Service* and you will get dozens of great ideas and lessons that you can put to use immediately."
— Shep Hyken, CSP, *Moments of Magic*

"*Celebrate Customer Service* gives you eleven great resources in one. Packed with thought-provoking and stimulating ideas, this book will convince you, beyond a shadow of a doubt, that thinking strategically about customer service really does pay."
— Nina Kawalek, Resource Center for
Customer Service Professionals

"It's really quite simple: To celebrate customer service you have to provide service worth celebrating. To offer—even revel—in such service, read this book!"
— Louis Patler, *Don't Compete . . . Tilt the Field*

"Among the key contributions of this fine book is that it takes the mystery out of what mystery shoppers really do, and how to use this technique to enhance customer service."
— Andrew J. DuBrin, *The Breakthrough Team Player*

Celebrate Customer Service

Insider Secrets

Featuring chapters by:

Joan E. Cassidy • Jeanette S. Cates • Rick Crandall
Mark Csordos • Theodore W. Garrison III
James Feldman • Sandra Livermon • Peggy Morrow
Edward J. Peters • Cindy Shaffer
Patricia Zakian Tith

Edited by Rick Crandall

Sponsored by
The Institute for Effective Sales and Marketing

Select Press
Corte Madera, CA

Select Press
P.O. Box 37
Corte Madera, CA 94976-0037
(415) 435-4461
SelectPr@aol.com

Other books in this series:
Celebrate Selling the Relationship-Consultative Way (1998)
Celebrate Marketing (1999)

Bulk sales/pricing available.

Celebrate Customer Service: Insider Secrets /
Rick Crandall (editor)

ISBN 1-890777-06-4

Printed in the United States of America
10 9 8 7 6 5 4 3 2 1

Contents

Preface

It seems like such a simple idea—great service makes for loyal customers and more profits.

But apparently it isn't so simple because many leading companies and business schools have decided that great service isn't worth the cost. But they don't understand lifetime value and the power of repeat business and referrals.

It's true that merely satisfied customers are not particularly loyal or profitable. But research by Bain, Xerox, and many others shows conclusively that really delighted customers are loyal. And retaining only 5% more customers can make up to a 75% difference in your profits, not to mention the value of their referrals.

So it's simple after all. Decide to give great service and create loyal customers. And invest in the tools like this book that will help you implement this "simple" idea at every level.

SECTION I
THE IMPORTANCE OF GREAT SERVICE

THE TRUE VALUE OF CUSTOMER SERVICE
Theodore W. Garrison III

SERVICE = MORE BUSINESS—REALLY!
Edward J. Peters

START WITH GREAT INTERNAL CUSTOMER SERVICE
FOR GREAT EXTERNAL CUSTOMER SERVICE
James Feldman

Chapter 1

THE TRUE VALUE OF CUSTOMER SERVICE

Theodore W. Garrison III

Theodore W. Garrison III works with contractors and related businesses that want to grow to the next level. He works both with individual companies and with trade associations and organizations that want to help their members. His programs focus on sales and marketing, customer service, leadership, and innovation in business.

He has more than 25 years of business, leadership, and motivation experience working in the construction and real estate development industries. He has held executive positions involved with the design, construction and marketing of almost a billion dollars worth of construction, including hotels, office buildings, and public facilities. He has been a licensed real estate broker since 1981. Garrison Associates provides individual counseling as well as seminars and keynote speeches to businesses and associations. His clients include Associated Builders and Contractors, Construction Management Association of America, and Skillpath. His talks are both informative and entertaining.

Garrison is a member of the National Speakers Association and the American Seminar Leaders Association. He has contributed chapters to *Marketing for People Not in Marketing* and *Celebrate Selling the Consultative-Relationship Way*.

Theodore W. Garrison, III, Garrison Associates, 900 W. Valley Road, Suite 201H, Wayne, PA 19087; phone (610) 341-8605; fax (610) 889-0901; e-mail garrison@bellatlantic.net.

THE TRUE VALUE OF CUSTOMER SERVICE

Theodore W. Garrison III

I have faith that the time will eventually come when employees and employers . . . will realize that they serve themselves best when they serve others most.

—B.C. Forbes, founder of *Forbes* magazine,
self-proclaimed "capitalist tool"

When a woman came into a Norwalk, Connecticut grocery store to buy a $40 tray of food for her afternoon function, the chef tried to convince her she was ordering insufficient food for 20 people. However, the lady resisted. Later that afternoon, the manager received a frantic phone call, "Why didn't you insist I buy more food? I'm going to run out!"

Now, what would you do? Well, the Stew Leonard's manager didn't hesitate. He quickly put together another $40 tray and personally rushed it out to the party and apologized for the inconvenience. He also told the lady it was free.

It just so happened those 20 guests were new real estate agents to the area. They were so impressed with the store's incredible service that they became regular customers and spent hundreds of dollars on groceries. And where do you think those agents tell their new home buyers they should buy their groceries?

This story, reported in *Inc.* magazine, demonstrates the value of great customer service. Stew Leonard's received thousands of dollars worth of benefits from a small $40 investment in customer service. It didn't matter that the lady was at fault. The manager recognized the opportunity and took advantage of it. What does your organization do with these "opportunities?"

* * * * *

Consider the following three questions about customer service.
- Why focus on customer service?
- What is great customer service?
- How does a company develop great customer service?

Every business—regardless of whether that business provides manufacturing, distribution, or services—must know and understand the answers to these questions in order to succeed.

This chapter will provide brief answers to these questions. Subsequent chapters will develop aspects of these themes in more detail, or will relate them to specific applications.

WHY FOCUS ON CUSTOMER SERVICE?

Different companies position themselves at both ends of the price spectrum—from the least expensive to the most expensive.

Companies make similar decisions about how to position themselves on the customer service

> Get the confidence of the public and you will have no difficulty getting their patronage.
> — H. George Selfridge

It's Not New, Folks

If you think customer service is a new concept, guess again. Peter Drucker in his book, *Management*, reports on Theodore N. Vail, the man who took Alexander Graham Bell's invention and turned it into the American Telephone and Telegraph Company (AT&T).

Almost 100 years ago, when Mr Vail was asked the question, "What is your business?" He responded, "Our business in service."

spectrum—from providing top-notch service and proclaiming it loud and clear, to ignoring customer service issues altogether. Unfortunately, most of these companies *say* they provide great customer service.

Yet, in your experience, how many companies have actually delivered great customer service? Polls indicate that very few do. And when companies promise to provide great service, but only give *lip service*, it hurts their reputations, their employees' attitudes, and their customers' trust.

We're All In the Service Business

A major factor contributing to a lack of customer service is that many businesses do not consider themselves in the service business. Their conclusion couldn't be further from the truth.

Regardless of your industry or the product you sell, you must understand you're actually in the service business! For example, two industrial giants of the early part of the 20th century, the steel industry and the railroad industry, did not think of themselves as service businesses. As a result, both experienced dramatic declines.

A Company that Caters to Its Customers

In contrast, in 1955 John H. McConnell started a new company called Worthington Steel by borrowing $600 at the time when the giants were beginning their decline. McConnell recognized that large mills were continuing to shift toward larger capacities with less and less flexibility—in other words, steel making on the manufacturer's terms.

So McConnell filled the gap for specialized orders and made steel on the customers' terms. Throughout its history, Worthington Industries from Columbus, Ohio, has emphasized customer service by providing solutions to problems instead of selling steel. While the giants of the industry declined—or went out of business—Worthington grew to be the largest independent steel processor in the U.S. with 1998 fiscal year sales over $1.6 billion.

A few years ago, I was involved in a series of projects on which Worthington Industries was a major supplier. I became concerned about some internal changes within their company and how they would affect the service we were receiving. I dropped their president, Donal Malenick, a brief note stating my concern.

A few days later, Mr. Malenick flew from Columbus to New Orleans and arrived on my doorstep with two of his senior vice presidents. They wanted to know what they needed to do to assure me that our needs would continue to be met as before. *That* is great customer service— especially when you consider I had not voiced a complaint, but merely a concern. Compare this to the way the steel mills or most businesses typically brush off real complaints. Is there any surprise that Worthington Industries continues to buck the decline of the big steel industry in the U.S.?

Customer Needs = Service Opportunities

If your company primarily provides services, it's obvious you're a service company. However, if you sell products, you are also in the service business. People don't buy your products, they buy the solutions or enjoyment those products provide. For example, IBM doesn't sell computers, they sell solutions to problems. It just so happens their solutions involve the use of computers.

Traditionally, people estimate that it is five times more profitable to sell to an existing customer than to a new customer. I suspect the ratio is closer to 20 times!
—Rick Crandall, *Marketing Your Services: For People Who Hate to Sell*

Peter Drucker said there are only two valid business purposes: to create customers and to innovate. Therefore, since you are in the service business and your goal is to create customers, it is pretty obvious that you are really in the customer service business! (There will be more about innovation later.)

Those businesses that don't deliver an acceptable level of customer service *during* the sales process quickly disappear because they lose too many sales. However, the more common problem is when a business stops delivering great service *after* the sale.

If your business falls into that group, the good news is you can survive. To do so, you must have a good system for generating new customers. Or your price must be cheap enough so that you can sell to the price shoppers.

The bad news is that you are unlikely to ever escape the survival stage of your business' development. Why? Because despite offering a product or service that customers want, by your actions you are forcing your business to operate within the lowest profit segment of your industry—the first sale. As long as you operate there, you can never truly be a successful business.

> Satisfied customers are an organization's most successful salespeople, because they do not stand to benefit financially from recommending the organization to others.
>
> —E.E. Scheuing, *Creating Customers for Life*

The Hard Facts

If you're still not convinced, look at the hard evidence. For years people have paid lip service to the importance of great customer service. But since service has not improved much in most businesses, we must assume people just don't believe the true impact of customer service on their business' bottom lines.

The Bain Consulting group has done some studies to place a dollar amount on the impact. They have learned that a mere 5% increase in customer retention can increase profits as much as 25% to 100%, depending upon the industry.

There are two important reasons for this exceptional result. First, it costs *at least* five times more in both time and money to generate a new customer than it does to gain repeat business or a referral. Second, when you deliver great, personalized customer service, you distinguish yourself from your competitors. This allows you to stop selling your product or service as a commodity. This is absolutely critical. When you sell a commodity, the primary distinguishing factor is price, which is probably the easiest and dumbest way to sell. If you sell by price, you must offer the lowest price, which is the least profitable way to run a business.

The Value of Customer Retention

Customer loyalty goes directly to your bottom line. Here are some figures for various industries:

Increase in Retention	Industry	Result
5%	Insurance	+60% profits
4%	Employer services (payroll, etc.)	+21% profits
5%	Banking	+40% profits
5%	Laundry	+60% profits

—Bain Consulting

False Referrals and Repeat Business

Another major problem with this approach is that despite your efforts to obtain these customers and service them, they only remain loyal until someone else offers them a lower price. You have "false" customers, so you don't get *profitable* repeat business and referrals.

When I tell clients or seminar attendees they must get more referrals and repeat business, many get defensive. They quickly point out they get repeat business and referrals. Of course, if you provide a quality product at a reasonable price, you probably will generate some referrals and repeat business. But what is the quality of your referrals and your repeat business?

Do your referrals consist of opportunities to bid your product or service to a new prospect? Is your repeat business generated by winning a bid over a group of other bidders for a client with whom you have previously worked? If this is your situation, then you are not really getting referrals and repeat business by my definition.

Keep the Focus on Service

When you have to bid for clients, you are merely selling your services as a commodity—maybe a quality commodity—but nonetheless a commodity. In the above cases, you are actually being selected based upon providing the lowest cost. There is little advantage in bidding to referrals or previous customers if the only criterion is price. In fact, the only advantage might be an easier time getting on the bid list. But once you are on the bid list, there is no advantage. In this kind of environment, it is virtually impossible to increase your profit margins. Instead, the competition is usually beating down those margins.

This is a certain path to destruction. As your profit margin drops, volume must increase to maintain the same gross profit. This creates additional stress on your organization, which increases overhead costs, thus requiring even further increases in volume to compensate for decreasing profits. The lifetime value of customers comes largely from their repeat business and referrals, *not* from their first purchase.

In his book *How to Sell at Prices Higher than Your Competitors,* my friend Lawrence L. Steinmetz prophesizes, "If you think you can match (or sell below) your competitor's prices, you need to understand that you will have an ongoing, lifetime gun battle of survival which, sooner or later, you are going to lose. There is nothing that is ever going to make that go away." Steinmetz's metaphor is an apt one. Competing on price is just like the gunslingers of the Old West: No matter how fast they were (or how low your price is), they eventually either slowed down enough or met someone even faster and they joined the other losers on Boot Hill. You can't afford to run your business that way.

Increase Profit Margins

So how do you increase profit margins?

By being the first and only choice of the customer. In many businesses, from construction to consulting, that means negotiating the work, instead of bidding it.

How do you earn that privilege? Simply stated, by distinguishing your business through great customer service.

Steinmetz suggested that there are basically five ways you can develop a competitive edge. His list included:

- price
- quality
- service
- advertising/promotions/salesmanship
- delivery

When handled correctly, all of the components on the above list are forms of customer service. Let's discuss each of these briefly.

Price. We have already talked about the down side of emphasizing price. But there is one exception. That is when you have a process or system that produces a product at less cost, thus saving your customers substantial amounts of money.

For example, Worthington Industries helped a U.S. rake manufacturer that was being hammered by overseas competi-

Service Tops Price in Where-to-Dine Decisions

EDK Forecast queried 500 executive women about their dining decisions. Seventy-nine percent said good service was their key criteria in restaurant selection.

In another study by MasterCard International, of the top ten reasons why diners say they choose one restaurant over another, six have to do with service, three with food, and only one with value.

tion. By adjusting the carbon content, Worthington was able to reduce the steel thickness. This modification resulted in sufficient savings for the rake manufacturer to be competitive with its overseas competitors. This was clearly a win-win situation. The rake manufacturer became more competitive in its marketplace. Worthington, despite reducing their price on the product, was able to increase their profit margin as result of the value they added. They also increased their volume because the rake manufacturer was selling more rakes. In the Worthington Industry case, the real competitive edge was service—customizing a product to a client's specific needs.

Quality. In today's marketplace, it is becoming harder and harder to distinguish yourself with quality. The reality is that without a quality product you won't even get a chance to play in the game. There are just too many alternatives for customers to choose from, so quality is a given. The real quality comes when you customize the product or service to the client's unique needs. This is also customer service. When you do this, you will have few, if any, competitors.

> Quality is never an accident; it is always the result of an intelligent effort.
> —John Ruskin

Advertising, promotion, and salesmanship. Advertising and promotion are the least tangible of the distinguishing characteristics. And they are the easiest to copy or duplicate. Of course, some large companies buy their market through extensive advertising and promotions. But, for most companies, this is not a viable approach.

If you don't deliver on the promises made in your advertising and promotions, you will only speed up your demise. Great salesmanship is really about providing one-to-one service to the customer. (For information about this concept, refer to another book in this series, *Celebrate Selling the Consultative-Relationship Way.*)

Delivery. Finally, there is delivery. This clearly is another form of customer service. Do you deliver your product or service on schedule and as promised? A publishing company gives the bulk of their printing jobs to one particular printer. (In fact, the publishing company often doesn't ask for a bid on the job.) Why do they give so much of their business to this particular printer when other printers would print the job to the same specifications at a lower cost? Because the printer *always* delivers the jobs on or before the due date. This allows the publishing company to meet its obligations. The publishing company also saves time by not shopping around and not having to keep close tabs on the printer to make sure the work gets finished when promised.

* * * * *

Lawrence Steinmetz could have changed the title of his list to "five ways to provide better customer service," because customer service is all there really is.

I realize that my analysis sounds simple, and I acknowledge that implementation is more difficult. But don't give up—the rest of this book is about how to do it.

WHAT IS GREAT CUSTOMER SERVICE?

Customer Service Is an Opportunity

As president of Scandinavian Airlines, Jan Carlzon turned the carrier around financially by emphasizing great customer service. In his book, *Moments of Truth,* he introduced the concept that each and every interaction with a customer is a "moment of truth." Each of these moments provides the opportunity to build customer confidence and trust—and conversely, the risk of diminishing confidence and trust. This includes moments that you might not even notice, such as a Web site that is annoyingly slow to load or that contains out-of-date information.

Quality in a service or product is not what you put into it. It is what the client or customer gets out of it.
—Peter Drucker

Satisfaction ≠ Loyalty

A one-point increase in satisfaction can mean a lot. Xerox found that customers who rated them a five instead of a four on a five-point satisfaction scale were *six times* more likely to buy more products! Unless customers *really* like you, they don't have much loyalty.

:_____:_____:_____✔:_____:_____:
Very   Very
dissatisfied   satisfied

Research by University of Texas Professor Robert A. Peterson highlighted a key aspect of customer loyalty. His research found *no* relationship between *good* customer service and customer loyalty. Only when emotion is injected into the equation does customer loyalty follow. He told me, "You must have your customers *love* you, and it is more important to manage customer expectations than to try to create perfect products." Fail to meet your customer's expectation during your "moments of truth," and you reduce your chances of referrals and repeat business.

Use *Customer* Definitions of Service

Every customer defines great customer service differently and each of their definitions is the correct one! Unless you understand this key concept, you will only deliver great customer service by luck. You must find out what is important to your customers.

The good news is that this provides you with unlimited potential to service your customers like no one else. Most of your competition won't take the time to find out what your customers' unique requirements and needs are, never mind take the time to address them.

In their book *Enterprise One to One*, Don Peppers and Martha Rogers delve into this concept in great depth. They advocate dealing with each customer on a one-to-one basis by providing customized service to meet each of their unique needs. Ideally, you would build a personalized interaction (relationship) with each customer. Once the customer has trained *you* properly (assuming you're trainable!), they won't want to invest the time to train one of your competitors, so you'll have an entrenched advantage.

You Can't Win an Argument With a Customer

The customer's perception is all that matters and you can't change that perception by arguing. Let me illustrate with an analogy. Instead of running your business, you decide to play a game of baseball. You are the batter and your customer is the umpire. A pitch comes in that is six inches off the plate, yet the umpire calls it a strike.

Is it a strike? Of course! The umpire called it a strike!

Should the pitch have been called a strike? That's another matter, but not relevant here. Can you change the call by arguing? Not only is the answer no, but if you argue too much, you're likely to get tossed out of the game!

In the business world, if you argue with your customer over her perception of the situation, you may not get fired on the spot, but you probably won't be given another chance. You'll be effectively tossed out of the business game.

HOW TO DEVELOP GREAT CUSTOMER SERVICE

You wouldn't have read this far if you didn't agree that great service is a worthy goal. But how do you really do it? Developing great customer service on a consistent basis requires the creation of a system. One approach to a system involves four steps:

- identify your "service difference"
- involve your customers
- experiment with new things
- build in flexibility

Your Service Difference

In their book *The Complete Idiot's Guide to Great Customer Service,* two friends of mine, Donald Blohowiak and Ron Karr, develop this important concept. They wrote, "The Service Difference is both the operating principles and the specific processes that combine to give your customers a warm feeling of satisfaction, maybe even joy, from interacting with your organization." Developing this Service Difference is absolutely essential because without it you are doomed to a struggling existence—if you survive at all. (In marketing, this is often called positioning.)

A perfect example is Kinko's copy centers. In the 1980s, they found themselves in a highly competitive commodity marketplace—photocopies. Complicating their marketplace was the fact that many such service businesses were highly specialized and targeted narrow niches. Kinko's competitors often cut prices on their single services in order to retain business, but Kinko's took a different approach. They recognized that most of their potential customers would rather have business services under a single roof, so they positioned themselves as the "small business branch office." This became their unique niche. The best part was they discovered that when you deliver what the customer wants, you don't have to compete on the price of your copies.

Where'd My Customers Go?

Michael LeBoeuf, in his book, *How to Win Customers and Keep Them for Life,* reports on a survey of why customers quit. He reports the following findings:

- 3% move away
- 5% develop other friendships
- 9% leave for competitive reasons (better prices)
- 15% are dissatisfied with the product
- 68% quit because of an attitude of indifference toward the customer by the owner, manager or some employee.

Ask Your Customers

So how do you find out what your customers want? The answer is simple: Ask them. This is more than a suggestion; it is a requirement. The truth of the matter is that only 4% of your dissatisfied customers will tell you they are unhappy, while 96% will just quietly leave. This results in your continuing to make the same mistakes and losing additional customers.

By regularly and frequently asking your customers what they think, you will at least eliminate your customer's perception of your indifference—the number one reason why customers quit.

To complete this phase, you must act on your customers' complaints or suggestions. Too often businesses respond that no one else provides that service, so why should we? Instead, accept the idea as an opportunity to distinguish your business from your competitors. The more of these unique services you provide, the easier it is to distinguish your business and stop selling a perceived commodity.

Address your customers' needs, not yours. *Inc.* magazine reported a story that supports this concept. A commercial building interiors contractor was struggling and decided to take a new approach. This contractor was finding it difficult to break into the bidding cycle with several building managers. So he went around and asked them, "What is your biggest problem with your current contractors?"

The building managers responded, "They are a mess. Their people are dirty and their clothes are tattered and they wear shirts with inappropriate slogans. They

Listen Directly to Customers

If you're not in regular contact with customers, spend one day a month in a customer contact position. For instance, Kevin Jenkins, president of Canadian Airlines, occasionally spends the day at a customer service counter. Jim Ryan, president of Canadian Tires Petroleum Division, spends occasional time pumping gas.

Benefits are twofold: They hear directly from customers and their appearances speak louder than words to employees about how these leaders value customer service.

make a mess of my lobby and elevator and they park their beat-up trucks in the front of the building. As a result, we're constantly receiving complaints from our tenants."

Our hero went back to his office and developed a new business plan that addressed the tenants' concerns. He put all his people into clean uniforms, which is what the service industry has done for years. He then provided his workers with vacuum cleaners and told them if you make a mess, clean it up immediately. And finally he told his people to park their trucks out of sight. He made his people invisible to the tenants.

The results were amazing. Suddenly his business was growing very rapidly despite the fact that he wasn't the cheapest contractor. The message is loud and clear—if you want customer loyalty, you need to address the client's issues, not yours.

Do more than just ask. Asking questions will only carry you so far. For your business to reach its full potential, it's essential that you:

- actively seek out your customers' problems and be flexible in acting on them
- find problems and needs your customers don't know they have

Each problem offers you an opportunity to distinguish your business from your competitors. Every time you provide something your competitors don't, you have added value to your service which customers will pay for.

Find New Needs

An individual inventor came up with the variable-speed windshield wiper now in use on all cars. When a major car company was asked why they hadn't developed it, their response was that customers had never asked for it!

Experiment, Experiment, Experiment

Customer service is only limited by your imagination and your ability to develop innovative solutions to your customers' problems. This is how you meet needs that customers don't know they have.

Using delivery to excel. Earlier, it was mentioned that Steinmetz identified delivery as a way to distinguish your business. A perfect example of providing extraordinary service through delivery is PSS/ World Medical. PSS provides medical supplies and equipment to physicians. It's not a glamorous business, or high tech. Yet the company grew from $90 million in sales in 1994 to over a $1 billion in sales three years later. When founder and CEO Patrick Kelly is asked to what he attributes their success, he offers two elements. First, he says you must understand your customers' business. Second, you must organize your business around what your customers value.

Kelly explains in his book that nurses usually order the supplies in doctors' offices. Sometimes the order is placed when a nurse goes into a drawer and finds it empty because someone forgot to order the item. PSS comes to the rescue because it guarantees same-day delivery if the order is placed by noon.

Hospitals have a different problem because they have large storage rooms. Their problem occurs when a piece of equipment breaks down. Imagine that you are responsible for the x-ray machine and it is scheduled solid for the entire day. Suddenly it breaks down. PSS guarantees they will have a technician at your location within two hours, while their competitors promise a re- sponse within 24–48 hours. Who would you call?

A major part of PSS's success is that they deliver what they promise—even when it's not profitable. In one situation, they had promised to deliver five pairs of crutches to a customer the next day, but then found out their supplier was out. So PSS ran all around town buying the necessary crutches at $30 a pair and then sold them to its customer the next day at $9 a pair. When asked about their actions, Kelly re- sponded, "I know its crazy, but the only thing that was impor- tant is that once you commit to a customer on your level of service, you've got to pay whatever the price to do it."

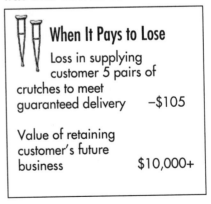

When It Pays to Lose

Loss in supplying customer 5 pairs of crutches to meet guaranteed delivery	–$105
Value of retaining customer's future business	$10,000+

Be Flexible

Often great customer service comes from being able to respond with flexibility to customers' immediate needs, or one of Carlzon's "moments of truth."

Time is money. For example, the monthly payment from the developer on a large hotel I was building in New Orleans was due on the Friday before a three-day weekend. The payment—for approximately $4 million—was to be made by a cashier's check. A few minutes before 5 p.m., I received a call from the developer's controller to come pick up our check. By contract they had to pay us on that day, but they had conveniently waited until after the local banks had closed to call me. They assumed this would allow them to continue to earn interest on the float over the three-day weekend.

I ran over to their office. Picked up the check. Ran back to my office. Next I called a bank officer I knew at the bank where my employer's local account was located. Despite the fact that First National Bank of Commerce was officially closed, the officer was still at her desk. I quickly explained that I had a cashier's check for $4,000,000 and would like it deposited immediately and included with Friday's deposits. She laughed and wanted to know if the check was made out to me. I told her that, unfortunately, it was to our company!

She said she could help me—even if it wasn't my money. The fact that the bank was already closed was no problem. When I arrived at the bank, a security guard let me in. I was met inside by the bank officer who assisted me through the deposit to insure that it was added to the already closed-out receipts for the day.

The next week, when I ran into the developer's controller, he asked, "How did you manage to

> I am a man of fixed and unbending principles, the first of which is to be flexible at all times.
> —Everett McKinley Dirkson

deposit the check before I gave it to you?" I just smiled and told him I had friends who could perform miracles. The bank's flexibility made me a hero with my employer. And where do you think I did my banking until I left New Orleans?

"I'm sorry, madam, but do you see service anywhere on the menu?"

An example of inflexibility. In contrast to the bank's flexibility, have you ever experienced a lack of flexibility by a business? For example, a friend of mine likes bacon, lettuce, and tomato sandwiches.

Several times at various restaurants, she has requested a BLT only to be told she couldn't order it because it wasn't on the menu. She would politely suggest that since toast, bacon, lettuce, and tomatoes were all ingredients in other menu items, that they must be available in the kitchen, and therefore they perhaps could be brought out together. Most servers would just shrug their shoulders and say it couldn't be done. Compare this to Friday's Restaurants whose policy is—if they have the ingredients, they will serve whatever you request. To which establishment are you most likely to return or refer your friends?

FOLLOW THE PLATINUM RULE

Most of us learned the "Golden Rule" while growing up. With regard to customer service, it's not good enough. Instead, we need to rely on the advise of author Tony Alessandra, who redefined the playing field with his "Platinum Rule"—namely, do unto your customers not what *you* would like, but what *they* want done unto them.

When all is said and done, customer service is the opportunity to add value to your business by providing innovative solutions for your customers' unique situations.

When you deliver great, one-to-one service for each customer, you make your customers more successful and happy. Your business is then more successful *and* more fun because we all enjoy interacting with very satisfied customers who can afford to pay us well. This book will give you many examples of how to achieve this ideal state, but getting started is up to you.

BURST INTO ACTION

The only measure of what you believe is what you do.

—Ashley Montagu

1 Determine what your real committment to great service is. Check with front-line people and customers to determine what is lip service and what is real.

2 Set up a simple system to gather customer input. If you already have a system, make sure that the information is being used.

3 Benchmark your service. Develop measurements you can track and compare to general service leaders in your industry and outside.

4 Measure the lifetime value of a customer to you.

5 Measure the percent of customers who are repeat and the number of true referrals you receive from them.

6 Experiment with some off-the-wall service ideas. Work to uncover needs customers don't know they have.

7 Make a list of ways you can use quality and delivery to make price unimportant to your customers.

8 Decide how you can use speed and flexibility to deliver better service than your competitors.

9 Determine what services customers will be happy to pay extra for.

10 Measure your customers' definitions of great service.

11 Develop a database of each major customers' specific concerns so you can deliver customized one-to-one service.

12 Look for even minor customer complaints and see if you can use them to thrill customers and turn these complaints into new standard procedures for great service.

SERVICE = MORE BUSINESS —REALLY!

Edward J. Peters

Edward J. Peters
is an entrepreneur, educator, speaker, and author in the world of relationship market-ing and customer satisfaction. He designs programs for getting and keeping customers, gives keynote speeches and seminars worldwide on "Getting 100% of the Business from 100% of Your Customers," and writes books including co-authoring *Marketing for People Not in Marketing.*

Mr. Peters has an extensive background in marketing and customer service including executive positions with one of the world's largest travel organizations. He served on the national advisory boards of three hotel chains and his customer communication programs were judged best in the nation by his peers. Some of his clients include Omni Hotels and Arlington International Racecourse, National Shoe Retailers Association, and the Inland Press Association.

Mr. Peters says that "you build business by building business relationships." As an outgrowth of that philosophy, his Relationship Marketing Institute Web site enables visitors to enjoy a new marketing or customer service idea every day. In addition, complimentary membership in the Institute to qualified business people entitles them to free marketing advice via phone or e-mail.

Ed Peters, Relationship Marketing Institute, 146 Second Street North, Suite 310, St. Petersburg, FL 33701; phone (727) 822-1272; fax (727) 822-1467; e-mail edpeters@100percentmarketing.com; www.100percentmarketing.com.

SERVICE = MORE BUSINESS —REALLY!

Edward J. Peters

> Sow good service; sweet remembrances will grow from this.
>
> — Madame de Stael

I t's no secret that customer service is in decline in the United States. According to the Better Business Bureau, complaints about customer service are up by 12% over the last five years and are now at an all-time high. Klaus Fornell, creator of the Customer Satisfaction Index at the University of Michigan, has been tracking customer service for four years and has seen a fairly steady decline in customer satisfaction.

Yet, Mark Baker, president of Home Depot, has said, "We believe it [customer service] is the only way to have profits in this business." Satisfied customers spend more money and come back more often! That's hardly a new notion. We all do business where we are known, respected, appreciated, and satisfied. We avoid doing business where we are merely a number, ignored, unappreciated, and unhappy.

They Think Great Service Is Unprofitable!

There certainly is a relationship between customer satisfaction and a healthy business. Surely all businesses know this. Or do they?

According to a report in October 1998 by Jim Avila of NBC Nightly News, ". . . at many business schools today . . . they teach that customer service may not pay at all. And they may be dying by design." Kristy Nordhem of Northwestern University says the lesson of the 1990s is that customer service is no longer important to the bottom line. "It's no longer the hot factor."

Customer-service tracker Fornell says, "Service is sacrificed for short-term profits. We have a current that is very dangerous . . . profits have been coming from cost-cutting for the most part. That's not sustainable in the long run."

Why do intelligent managers, executives, and shop owners believe that delighting customers doesn't pay? Perhaps it's because most businesses don't measure the value of positive word-of-mouth advertising. The retailer Nordstrom is a service legend because they encourage stories of extravagant customer service. It may cost them a few dollars more to provide the ultimate in customer service, but the increased business from word-of-mouth tales of their service is worth millions.

> Great industries are not built up by getting the best of someone else, but by giving goods and services that are worth more to your customers than the amount they pay you in return.
> —G. Heath Clark

WHAT'S CUSTOMER SATISFACTION WORTH?

Customer satisfaction isn't just about making customers feel good, but about getting them to interact with the business more often, spending more money when they do. Sounds reasonable, doesn't it? And yet, in more than twenty-five years of working with hundreds of companies on their marketing, I have found very few who understand this simple equation:

Delighted Customers = More Business

Large companies have long tried to correlate customer service to sales revenue. The Marriott Corporation has said that a 1% increase in customer satisfaction at its hotels is worth more than $50 million in sales. At just one IBM assembly plant, a 1% increase in customer satisfaction is reported to be worth more than $275 million over five years.

Surprisingly, however, the relationship of customer satisfaction to sales isn't only revealed when we compare good to bad service.

Good vs. Bad Service

The relationship between good and bad service and sales is evident in small companies as well. For one of my clients, a downtown Chicago hotel, the difference between a guest having a bad versus good experience translated to over 7,000 fewer room nights a year, or nearly $1 million dollars in lost sales.

CUSTOMER SATISFACTION IS WORTH MILLIONS

In my chapter, "Get 100% of the Business from 100% of Your Customers," in the book *Marketing for People Not in Marketing*, I told the story of a client, a large Chicago-based men's clothing store, whose profits rose $1.2 million because the store owners understood the relationship between customers "loving" them and customers "liking" them.

Over 60,000 customers (nearly the entire customer list) were surveyed and asked, among other things, to describe their overall experience with the store. Nearly 10,000 customers responded. Forty-eight percent of the respondents described their experiences at the store as excellent, 49% described their experiences as good, and 3% described their experiences as fair or poor.

Tracking store visit frequency and the amount of money each customer spent at each visit, we found the following, incredible result: Customers who had an "excellent" shopping experience visited the store an average of 3.9 times a year and spent an average of $465 per visit. Customers who merely had a "good" experience visited the store 3.5 times a year and spent only $397 per visit. The difference between a "great" and a "good" experience was nearly half a visit per year and $68 spent per visit . . . or a difference of $3.2 million in lost sales.

BETTER SERVICE = MORE INCOME!

In the previous book, I reported that, through a series of customer satisfaction improvements we recommended and implemented over an eighteen month period, the percentage of customers who reported an excellent experience grew from 48 to 62! Sales increased by $1.2 million!

The original survey we conducted grew out the store owner's fear of increased competition from new men's clothing stores opening in Chicago. My firm, the Relationship Marketing Institute, was approached by the store's owners to develop a marketing plan to fend off the new competition.

My observation was that the competition was better known and better financed and would be worthy opponents in finding and attracting *new* customers, the client's stated objective. I believed the client was better positioned to grow their business with *existing* customers and recommended the survey to uncover untapped sales potential within this group.

Our client was surprised to learn that 97% of his customers had a positive experience in his store. Relieved that it wasn't lower, he nearly abandoned the idea of focusing his marketing on existing customers. That was until I communicated a most powerful observation to my client — "Ninety-seven percent of your customers like you, but only 48% of them love you." And as we have reported, the difference between "love" and "like" was amazingly significant.

"SHARE OF CUSTOMERS"

Not only did the survey uncover the correlation between customer satisfaction and sales potential, but it also revealed an untapped gold mine of existing customer market penetration.

We asked customers if they did all their men's clothing shopping at our client's store and only 9% said they did. When we asked this group the reasons for their loyalty, they responded with "price" and "selection." This made sense because the store was known for its low prices and its huge selection, and all its marketing and advertising focused on these attributes.

In obtaining high levels of customer satisfaction, it makes little difference what we do, but rather, how our customer perceives what we've done.

When we asked why the 91% "shopped around," they reported, to our client's dismay, "price" and "selection."

I jokingly asked my client if he increased prices for some customers and whether he hid merchandise from others. His reaction was typical: "How can our customers not understand that

---

Talk to Customers

Call several customers each week. If possible, find one who's satisfied, one who's dissatisfied, and one who's in the middle. Another way to do this is to take random customer calls during the week yourself. This gives you a good feel for what the people who use your products and services are really concerned about.

—*The Marketing Report*

we have the lowest prices in the Midwest and that we carry more brands than anybody else?"

Apparently, a large group of customers knew little about the store's pricing, selection, and competitiveness. We immediately recommended a new price tag that showed both the store's discounted price and the price at a local department store. Additionally, merchandise that had been scattered randomly throughout the store was better positioned, grouped by brand, and, in some cases, better illuminated. We created a newsletter for the store that focused on communicating the store's commitment to low prices and big selection.

```
List Price
 $399.95

Our Price
 $249.95

You save
 $150.00
```

SATISFACTION COMMISSIONS

One of the most effective strategies we implemented was to take the salespeople off "sales" commissions and put them on "satisfaction" commissions. Each time customers indicated on the customer satisfaction survey that they had an "excellent" experience at the store, and gave the clerk's name, they earned $5.00. Each time a customer referred to a salesperson and reported a "good," "fair," or "poor" experience, $5.00 was deducted from the commission pool. The objective was to give the customer an "excellent" experience every time, and salespeople were given incentives to make it happen.

The "excellent" and "good" experiences described by customers had little to do with a traditional notion of customer

> ### Paying for Service
>
> The idea of rewarding salespeople for improving customer service is becoming more and more popular. Sears, Roebuck & Company is testing a system to link as much as 10% of pay (up or down) to customer satisfaction measured through surveys.

service. Instead, they were based on perceptions—how the store lived up to its promise of delivering a huge selection of merchandise at low prices.

Our client's competitors spent large amounts beating each other up looking for new customers. Our client focused on increasing sales by improving customer satisfaction among its most valuable asset—its existing customers.

THE CORRELATION HOLDS!

Whenever we compare customer satisfaction to revenue, the results are always the same. The higher the level of customer service, the more the businesses are rewarded with increased sales.

At a large suburban Chicago custom art framing shop, customers who reported their overall satisfaction as excellent spent an average of $404 a year on framing. Customers who reported a mere good overall experience spent only an average of $264 a year—a huge difference. In those rare cases where customers reported fair or poor satisfaction, they spent only an average of $73 and $15 a year respectively.

Because the difference between a great and a good experience was so significant, we surveyed each customer to determine what made some of them love their experience and some of them only like it. The results were overwhelming: "Give us more frames from which to select!"

The problem wasn't with our client's inability to choose frames its customers would purchase, but rather with a space limitation in which to display samples. Our client's solution—get rid of store space being used to display seldom-purchased and unprofitable merchandise and remodel the space to house the hundreds of frame samples customers clamored for.

When the remodeling project was complete, we designed a picture postcard of the "new" space.

We sent it to all existing customers and invited them to visit what had become, because of what they told us, the largest selection of custom art frames on the north shore of Chicago.

GOOD SERVICE ISN'T ENOUGH

The difference between liking and loving a business can be as simple as who paid the most attention to you when you needed them the most.

Needs Analysis Is as Basic as Courtesy

Recently, I called two distributors of video projection equipment whose ads appeared in the monthly magazine of the National Speaker's Association. I explained that I was a professional speaker in the market for projection equipment.

The first call was handled by a extremely courteous receptionist who enthusiastically took my name and address and promised to send me her company's catalog.

The second call was passed from the receptionist to a salesperson who asked me fourteen questions including, "What size audience do you typically speak to?", "Will you be traveling with your video projector?", and "What software will you run on your laptop?" His final question was "What is your address?" and he ended the conversation with "Based on what you've told me, I know what to recommend that you purchase and I'll mail you the information."

Within a few days, two envelopes arrived. The first, from the courteous, enthusiastic receptionist, contained a catalog with twelve models from which I could choose. The second contained a letter from the

> VIDEO PROJECTION
> NEEDS ANALYSIS
>
> 1. How many times each month will you need to use the projector?
>
> 2. What size audience do you typically speak to?
>
> 3. What software do you use?
>
> 4. Do you need to travel with your projection equipment?

salesperson which said, "Based on your answers to my questions, I recommend either of two of our models from the eleven we sell and I've enclosed the two pages from our catalog that describe them."

Where would you purchase your video projector? If you were a member of a large, national speaker's association, how many colleagues would you send to the salesperson who delivered the highest level of customer service by asking you those fourteen questions?

IT'S THE MISSED OPPORTUNITIES THAT HURT MOST

My experience with the video projection companies leads me to an important aspect of correlating customer satisfaction to sales: Much business is lost not just because of poor service but because we miss bona fide opportunities to close a sale and satisfy a customer.

Poorly handled inquiries can be looked at as both poor service and poor salesmanship. They are missed sales opportunities.

I received a call once from a person from Minolta wanting to know if I was happy with my copier. I explained that I used the copier of my office neighbor across the hall and they used my fax machine in return. The caller said, "Thank you," and just hung up. If she had asked for the name and number of my office neighbor, I would have gladly told her his copier was constantly breaking down and was in dire need of replacement.

Lost Opportunities

Marketing News, a trade publication, made 5,000 telephone calls to retail Yellow Pages advertisers requesting price information on a particular product. The results are evidence of lost sales opportunities:

- 56% did not answer the phone in the first eight rings
- 8% put the caller on hold for more than two minutes
- 11% could not provide the information requested
- 31% provided only the price and then hung up
- 78% never even asked for the caller's name

FOLLOW-UP IS KEY: "BANK ON IT"

Many sales are lost before we have even had a chance to be satisfied by a business.

Just prior to moving my business to St. Petersburg, Florida, from Lake Forest, Illinois, I telephoned six banks whose names I got from the St. Petersburg Chamber of Commerce membership directory. With each call, I explained the following:

- that I was moving my personal, corporate, and father's estate checking and savings accounts to St. Petersburg within a month (and I revealed the value of each account)
- that as the immediate past president of my local Chamber of Commerce, I was giving them an opportunity to have my business because they were St. Petersburg Chamber members
- that I wished to receive by mail, specific services offered by the bank and a list of specific fees I might have to pay, if any.

Four of the banks never sent me anything! The two that did sent only their standard marketing materials with no specific product or cost information I had requested. But I needed a bank so I decided to give the two banks that responded a second chance.

Both banks this round told me of specific people who handled relocations. None of the six banks mentioned this the first time around. One of the bank's relocation people returned my call, got my voice mail, promised to call back the same afternoon . . . and never did.

The other bank's relocation person returned my call within two hours, spent 40 minutes on the phone with me, outlined all my benefits for doing business with her bank, answered all my questions and even arranged a conference call at the bank's expense with the trust department to discuss concerns I had about my father's estate accounts.

Any guesses as to where I do my banking in St. Petersburg? Businesses spend huge amounts of money hoping their phones will ring with new business and, when they finally do, they drop the ball.

If your business doesn't have a system to track and follow up inquiries, you are missing out. You won't know if you're missing 10% free extra business—or 100%—if you don't measure it.

LOSING BUSINESS THAT FALLS RIGHT IN YOUR LAP

The other thing I did before moving to St. Petersburg was to send a personalized letter to 600 Chamber of Commerce businesses to introduce myself and the Relationship Marketing Institute. I enclosed a form and a postage-paid envelope readers could use to indicate their interest in my consulting services, speeches and seminar offerings, and my previous book. I was delighted to hear from 1.3%, or eight, of the businesses.

Hello—
I'm moving to your area and want to do business with you.
Please use the enclosed postage-paid envelope to send me information about your business.

U.S. Postage Paid

But I had also invited all 600 businesses to use my postage-paid envelope to send me information about their companies. I only heard from one! I explained that as a new resident and business in town, I would need to purchase many products and services, and that as a rule, I try to do business with fellow Chamber of Commerce members (I had already joined the Chamber and said that in the letter). Despite all that, 599 businesses passed on the opportunity to get me as a new customer at no cost!

I tell both of these stories to incredulous business owners in my speeches throughout St. Petersburg. Audiences can't believe that businesses could be so stupid and yet in one audience of thirty disbelievers, four were people I had written to only months before!

FINAL PROOF THAT SERVICE EQUALS PROFITS

Lack of attention to the perils of poor customer relationships is endemic to entire industries.

Prior to conducting a day-long marketing and customer satisfaction seminar for a nationwide group of hobby shop owners, I did a bit of research. I wanted to get a sense of the current climate related to customer satisfaction in the independent hobby shop industry. The hobby shop trade publication that sponsored my seminar conducted a survey of 200 hobby shop owners and found that only 43% thought marketing was important. A broad definition of marketing is anything you do to get or keep a customer. Did hobby shop owners also think customer service was not that important?

Good will plus good service brings sales success that no competition can possibly undersell.
—Harry F. Banks

Customers Don't See It Your Way

Not convinced that hobby shops were immune to the benefits of innovative marketing and good customer service, I dug a little deeper. I found a survey the industry conducted of the customers of 503 hobby shops. The main reasons customers listed for visiting hobby shops were looking for supplies, seeing new products, help, and service. The reasons hobby shops got people through their doors were the very things customers felt most dissatisfied with. Not one category of customer satisfaction (cleanliness, courtesy, customer service, expertise, selection, and new products) had even half the respondents rating services as excellent.

I Become an Informal Mystery Shopper

Still refusing to believe that I was about to speak to owners in an industry out-of-touch with even basic customer satisfaction strategies, I personally and anonymously visited several hobby shops. (See Chapter 4 for more on formal mystery shopping.)

At one shop I found a huge model train display whose track layout ran throughout the store. It was clearly set up for customer trial. However, none of the four trains on the track were operable.

At another store, the large display windows had tables in front of them that were used to pile up cardboard boxes. These unattractive piles of boxes were clearly visible from the outside. At that same store, I heard a customer holding an item ask an employee, "What if I get home and I can't figure this thing out?" The employee responded, "The instructions are in the box."

At virtually every store, merchandise was piled so high on shelves that Shaquille O'Neal couldn't have reached it.

Bad Service Was the Norm

One store was located at the end of a one-way dead-end street in an obscure neighborhood. You had to make a real effort to find it. In other words, these guys didn't get a lot of drive-by or walk-in traffic. And yet, I was allowed to browse the store for forty minutes before anyone spoke to me.

Lost sales abounded at my visits. In one store, I asked the salesperson (later discovered to be one of the owners) if they had any P-47 aircraft merchandise (my father's unit in WWII). He said the only thing they had on P-47s was a book which I eventually took to the cash register to purchase.

While the $10 book was being rung up, I noticed a huge remote-controlled P-47 airplane on top of a ten-foot high shelf. I asked to see it, shied away from its $150 price, and bought only the book.

Guess what? I'm very interested in P-47 merchandise but that hobby shop can't take advantage of that valuable information because no one got my name or wrote down anything about my P-47 interest.

The big model plane had a thick layer of dust on it and the colorful box was a bit faded. I suspected it had been atop the high shelf for a long time. I wonder if I could have been persuaded to upgrade my purchase if someone had described the plane's merits or sent me a note a week later with a discount coupon?

I left the store with my $10 book thinking about those 43% of hobby shop owners who apparently thought marketing wasn't important.

What Can You Do to Make Sure Your Customers Receive Great Service?

Providing great customer service isn't that difficult or costly. It's mostly a matter of setting expectations and rewarding good behavior. Consider the following:

- Set customer service goals (for example, point out the location of sales merchandise to all customers).
- Write mini-scripts for what you want employees to say in specific situations (initial greeting, when you don't have what the customer is looking for, and so forth). Employees should be allowed to use their own words if they wish, as long as they retain the tone and meaning of the original message.
- Keep a customer service policy binder containing the expectations and scripts, so employees can refer back to them as needed.
- Display letters and comments about great customer service.
- Praise employees when you see them doing well.
- Budget $100 a month to reward employees. Hand a $20 bill to an employee who has provided exceptional service.

CONCLUSION

In case after case, we see significant correlations between delighted customers and increased sales, and how the lack of customer satisfaction results in missed sales opportunities. It has become increasingly obvious that the better we can satisfy our customers, before, during, and after the sale, the more business we can expect to get.

Despite the hard evidence cited in this book, most companies, unfortunately, still don't believe in investing in great service. On a recent plane flight, I met a gentleman seated next to me and we began discussing customer satisfaction. He mentioned that his company, a large manufacturer and distributor of mobile telephone equipment, was actually considering deliberately reducing customer satisfaction because they couldn't afford it! Let's hope your competitors feel the same way!

BURST INTO ACTION

The people who get on in this world are the people who get up and look for the circumstances they want, and if they can't find them, they make them!

—George Bernard Shaw

If we agree that increased customer satisfaction equals more business, what are some of the things you can do to increase satisfaction?

1 Measure customer satisfaction! You can't improve on it if you don't know your starting point.

2 Use innovative relationship marketing and unprecedented customer service to increase customer satisfaction.

3 Include your employees in customer service changes. Enlist their ideas.

4 Consider paying specific bonuses or commissions for high customer ratings.

5 Understand that every aspect of every customer interaction is an opportunity to get more business . . . or lose it. Make a list of your "moments of truth" when prospects and customers form impressions of you.

6 Know your customers . . . what do they want from your business? What do they like about you; what do they dislike?

7 Use the information you learn about your customers to build a relationship with each customer. Keep track of what you know in a database.

8 Work to reward loyal customers and encourage referrals.

START WITH GREAT INTERNAL CUSTOMER SERVICE FOR GREAT EXTERNAL CUSTOMER SERVICE

James Feldman

James Feldman
is the president of several
marketing companies that
specialize in promotions utiliz-
ing both merchandise and travel incentives.

He has earned the recognition of his peers becoming the only person in
the motivation industry to earn both the CITE (Certified Incentive Travel Executive)
and MIP (Master Incentive Professional) designations.

Mr. Feldman is a frequent speaker, internationally, on customer service
programs through Shift Happens!® Inc. He has written over 100 articles on
motivation, learning from his clients that include Toyota, Mary Kay Cosmetics,
Apple, Subaru, Otis Sauder, Compaq, Clairol, Frito-Lay, and Volkswagen.

James Feldman, Shift Happens!® Seminars, Inc., 505 North Lake Shore Drive
#6601, Chicago, IL 60611; phone (312) 527-9111; fax (312) 527-9112;
e-mail Shift Hpns@aol.com; Internet http://www.shifthappens.com.

START WITH GREAT INTERNAL CUSTOMER SERVICE FOR GREAT EXTERNAL CUSTOMER SERVICE

James Feldman

> The key to great customer service is a satisfied employee.
>
> —Roger Dow, Marriott Hotels and Resorts

I was on board a Carnival cruise to the Caribbean. Within an hour after departure, we ran into a rainstorm. There was nothing to do but go back to the cabin. I turned on the TV to find that it did not work. The radio did not work. I called the cabin steward and was directed to the engineer. He informed me that due to the storm, he could not come to the cabin for an hour or two. After putting down the phone, I decided to read a book. The phone rang. It was the purser. He apologized for the delay, apologized for the nonavailability of the engineer, and offered to move me to another cabin. I explained that I was fine but that I appreciated the call. Ten minutes later, the cabin steward was at my door asking if the TV had been fixed. When I explained the situation, he offered to move me to another cabin, if only to be able to watch TV.

Almost as quickly as the rain started, it stopped. I went to dinner. Upon my return, I found a handwritten note from the television technician. He explained that the fuse in my cabin had been replaced and everything was now working. He left his beeper number in case I needed him again. While reading his note, a letter was slipped under my door. It read "Mr. Feldman, I have been unable to reach you this evening by phone. My service technician informs me that he has repaired your television and radio. If, for any reason, they are not working, please call me at my direct extenson." I was amazed.

No Problem Is Small to the Customer

Here was a small problem—certainly not one that required phone calls and handwritten notes. And while I fully appreciated their attention to my problem, on a larger scale, the crew's response spoke volumes for the training that Carnival provides to their thousands of employees.

I sat down and wrote a note to Robert Dickenson, president of Carnival. As I was sealing the envelope, I heard a knock at the door. It was the cabin steward with a bottle of champagne, a fruit and cheese platter, and a note from the captain of the ship. The captain apologized for the inconvenience and hoped that my cruise would be "more than I expected" for its duration. It was. I told dozens of people about my experience. Carnival became my most utilized and recommended cruise line. And, of course, I booked another "sail" with them.

In whatever you do—whether it's the service you provide or the way you set up your office—make sure there is a 'wow factor,' something that will grab people's attention and make them notice that you've sweated the details.
—Carl Sewell, *Customers for Life*

Focus Job Descriptions on Outcomes

You can make simple changes in job descriptions to improve internal customer service. For example, "filing" should be called "document retrieval" instead. What good does it do if a secretary spends time filing, but is then unable to find things when they're needed.

Job descriptions and evaluations should focus on desired outcomes. This will help employees understand *why* they need to do certain things, show them how their jobs help others, and allow them to contribute to the bigger whole.

—Ken Blanchard
("The One Minute Manager")

Carnival's Great Responses

None of this could have happened without the training, co-worker involvement, and overall organizational goal of customer satisfaction. No one blamed the other person. Everyone acted like a team member. Everyone understood the role of others. It was truly a fantastic example of how to empower employees with internal customer service training that resulted in superior external customer service.

The other chapters in this book focus on external customers, without whom you couldn't survive. Many of the principles of customer service discussed in these chapters also apply to internal service issues. This chapter focuses on internal customers—your employees—without whom you also can't survive as an organization. Great customer service must be a total commitment from your company. And every employee is also a customer.

EMPLOYEES AS CUSTOMERS

Internal customers are your co-workers. A company that understands how to expand the knowledge, commitment, and satisfaction of internal customers will create happy external customers.

Employees are often each other's customers at different times. For example, managers have to report payroll numbers properly—and on time—for the payroll department to do their job. In turn, the payroll department issues accurate checks, on time, for managers as well as other employees.

You are the customer of people who work for you because you're dependent on them to do your job. And they are also your customers because they depend on you for information, training and support.

Benefits of Satisfied Employees

Co-workers must interact before they can act on behalf of a customer. If the interaction is not positive, it's much harder to give the external customer a positive customer service experience.

A dissatisfied employee:

- costs the company money
- gives poor customer service
- recruits others to the "dark side"
- bad-mouths your company to your customers

Having happy employees translates to great customer service for at least three reasons:

- Happy employees like their jobs and project that attitude to customers.
- They want the company to succeed and realize that taking care of customers is the best way to insure that.
- You are a role model for others—when you treat others with respect and show them that you care, it helps them see how to treat customers the same way.

Value Your Employees

If you could not advertise in any manner—no television, radio, newspapers, promotional literature, or billboards—and your customers could not visit your property, see pictures, or talk to other customers, then what is left? Your employees! What would the employees say about your company? Are you confident that the information would be favorable? Would you lose business? Would you gain business? Do your employees understand the importance of keeping your existing customers?

Reward Internal Service

In most cases, a good internal customer service program can be achieved by education. If you are encouraging employees, you are developing their skills and self-esteem which increases their

Frontline Employees Are an Organization's Foundation

Jan Carlzon, author of *Moments of Truth*, suggests turning the organizational pyramid upside-down. When you put external customers at the top of the pyramid, then it becomes clear that the frontline people are the most important in your organization, and it's everyone else's job—especially top execs—to support them.

CUSTOMERS

Your Front Line

Supervisors

Managers

VPs

CEO

value to your organization, thereby increasing their value to your customers.

Employees must work together to form a cohesive unit that can service the customers of a business. Workplace conditions, education, and empowerment all contribute to satisfied internal customers. A simple thank you between employees or supervisors can go a long way. But, internal politics can kill external service.

Your company may be able to give good service without an internal focus, but you will never get your employees to go the extra mile unless they want to do so. "Yes" must replace "no." "Can do" must replace "not my job."

GREAT INTERNAL SERVICE TRANSLATES TO GREAT EXTERNAL SERVICE

In an attitude survey by Watson Wyatt Worldwide, well over 80% of 9,144 polled respondents said they know their employer's goals and their duties. But 38% said they needed information or regular feedback. And only 55% have the power to make decisions to satisfy customers.

Based on these responses, where do you think you should focus your efforts on keeping customers happy?

What Do Employees Want from Their Jobs?

An old sales rule states, "When customers tell you what they want, give it to them." Translate this rule to your organization: "If we know what an internal customer wants, we will provide it."

We know that a people-approach to business results in profits. Many studies have shown that money is not the biggest motivator for employees. But most bosses still find this hard to understand.

Look at the box to see what employees want in their jobs—and what supervisors think

What Employees Want in Their Jobs: Rankings by Employees and Supervisors		
	EMPLOYEES	SUPER-VISORS
Interesting work	1	5
Appreciation	2	8
Feeling "in" on things	3	10
Job security	4	2
Good pay	5	1
Promotions	6	3
Good working conditions	7	4
Personal growth	8	7
Help/personal problems	9	9
Tactful discipline	10	6

—George Mason University Survey

employees want. Note the big discrepancy between employees' top three wants and supervisors' ratings of their importance.

What Great Internal Customer Service Means

The objectives of great internal customer service are to:

1. *retain* existing employees and encourage them to "come back" to work each day. (Happier employees also save you money and perpetuate a positive culture by recruiting new applicants with similar attitudes and expectations.)
2. increase the *awareness* of each employee of the need for dedication to exceeding co-worker expectations.
3. increase the *commitment* of each person to be responsible for co-worker satisfaction; to revise policies and procedures whenever necessary to increase overall satisfaction.

A satisfied employee will create and keep satisfied customers. A dissatisfied employee will cost you customers.
—Michael Le Boeuf, *How To Win Customers and Keep Them for Life*

4. *empower* each employee with information and decision-making authority.
5. make the workplace a positive place.

Putting Customers Second

Howard Schultz, the head of Starbucks, feels that part of his secret to success is to cultivate customer contentment by exalting his employees:

Our people come first, then the customers, then the shareholders. It may sound out of order, but we can't exceed the expectations of our customers unless we exceed it for our employees first.

We often forget that our employees are also our customers. We are selling them on the premise that we are a good company with a valuable product, offered at a fair price. We treat our customers fairly—now we need to apply that principle to our employees.

The best employees can be described as:

- trustworthy
- relationship oriented
- solution-minded
- advocates for customers
- action-oriented (look for chances to help other employees and customers; see also Chapter 11)

On the other side are the less productive employees who are:

- never satisfied with the job, company, or pay
- always want to change the rules to suit themselves; political
- getting by with the minimum, never volunteer

Internal Customer Service Skills

- ability to identify internal customer needs
- active listening skills
- problem-solving skills
- conflict-handling skills

- offer "acceptable" feedback, not real comments
- have one foot out the door; always looking for a deal
- reactive

Again, a simple truth explains it all: "Do unto others as you would have them do unto you." Treat each employee as an appreciating asset.

New World Library is an example of a company that has real values and strong internal and external customer service programs. The owner, Marc Allen, believes in sharing, as described in one of his books. He splits profits with employees 50/50! Last I checked, their company had about 10 employees and about $15 million in sales. Their sales per employee are among the highest in the country—higher than Microsoft's. And their profit margins mean that employees share hundreds of thousands of dollars every year. You can bet that employees work with each other to better serve customers. And their workforce is extremely stable, making it easier to maintain good relationships with customers, suppliers, authors, and other constituencies.

Benefits of Employee Satisfaction

Companies that have distinguished themselves in the way they hire, train, and treat employees have experienced the following positive benefits.

- increases in service, quality, and customer satisfaction of over 50%
- growth rates 60% to 300% greater than their competition
- return on sales 200% to 300% greater than their competitors
- return on assets 150% to 300% greater than their competitors
- direct impact on employee retention which in turn leads to customer satisfaction which leads to profits

—William Fromm,
*The Ten Commandments of
Business and How to Break Them*

IMPROVING INTERNAL CUSTOMER SERVICE

To create a great service culture, recognize that employees have practical power. They do not have to go the extra mile. They do not have to interact with others in a supportive fashion. They understand what minimum performance is expected and determine, on their own, how much more to give.

If you want to truly get the most out of employees, you must "enlist" them everyday by educating, marketing, and publicizing the fact that your company is worthy of their efforts. When your company does something above the norm, let everyone know.

The steps necessary to create a strong internal service culture are the same general steps necessary to create any organizational change. There needs to be a sustained effort from the top that recruits employees to make the necessary efforts to implement a new "culture." (See also Chapter 9.)

Here is an outline of the steps to increase your internal customer satisfaction.

Communicate a Clear Vision and Specific Goals

Every change program must have a clear vision and specific goals that are repeatedly communicated to employees. Focusing on external customer service is an excellent key to change. Employees understand its importance. When an organization is in crisis, it can usually be saved by more business from customers. Even in nonprofit organizations, employees can easily see that if customers aren't happy, their jobs will not be secure.

Internal customer service is also a message employees will resonate to because it's for them. Most companies try to motivate change in order to be more "effi-

---

Calling Employees to Service

A medical equipment company was growing fast. People with different management skills were being hired. The company president heard that some people weren't being treated well. He knew that the success of the company depended on internal cooperation, that success required a careful synchronization between sales and service and a real caring for customers. He issued a "Call to Service":

When dealing with people, recognize: *every* person as your customer, *every* task as your service, and *exceeding* expectations as your goal.

Everyone received training to learn how to better serve customers, both internal and external.

Among the many company awards given is the CEO's Award for Excellence that is awarded to the person who has most exceeded the expectations of internal or external customers.

cient." This not only has little personal appeal for employees, it often threatens them (read "downsizing coming"). By pairing internal and external service, you have a strong message that employees will buy into.

Involve Employees

By obtaining employee input early, you will not only get ideas, you will reduce resistance to change. When they are involved in creating the program, they will be more committed to carrying it out.

Repeat Your Message

The more employees understand their importance within the organization, and their personal contributions to making the workplace more productive, the better your chance of increasing the cooperative interaction of each co-worker.

> ### Frontline Employees Are an Organization's Foundation
>
> Too few top executives go out and work on the front lines to get a feeling for what customer interaction is like.
>
> An often overlooked benefit of executives spending time on the frontlines is that they get feedback from their own employees ("customers"). For instance, when Anheuser-Busch execs ride along in the beer delivery trucks, not only do they hear from their customers, but it's also a chance to find out what the delivery people need to make their jobs easier.

It is natural to resist something we do not understand. Repetition of an internal service message helps reduce the resistance which leads to a more cohesive effort to achieve established goals.

Ask Co-Workers to Resolve Their Problems Themselves

If you are trying to build a bridge between co-workers, allow them to fix any problem that arises immediately. The interaction can create a better understanding of procedures and policies that will foster a "team effort." Co-workers best relationships are personalized. Empower employees. Treat them like adults. Suggest that they are the caretakers of the company.

Create Clear Rewards

What are you doing to focus on appreciation of employees' work? People like to be recognized. They love to be recognized in front of their peers. Make recognition part of every program that is run by your company, no matter how small the actual prize.

Build Excitement

Make new programs fun. Create a game with points where everyone can win. Make the timing build to a crest that can sustain culture change.

SERVICE IS A VIRTUOUS CYCLE

The final result of great internal customer service is the ability of your company to attract, keep, and satisfy long-term employees. Customers appreciate stability in the people they deal with so this furthers organizational success. This, in turn, makes it easier to reward and keep employees. To get started, create a program with clear rewards.

The strength of Marriott's teamwork ethic simply means that we've successfully created an environment in which the rewards for working together outweigh those of working for one's own interest.

—Bill Marriott,
The Spirit To Serve

USING INCENTIVES TO CREATE GREAT INTERNAL SERVICE

In his book *Outrageous Service,* T. Scott Gross says that all labor is emotional labor. He reports that a survey of managers estimated that motivated employees would be 30% more productive than those who were not motivated.

This may be an underestimate. Greg Steltenpohl, a founder of the fresh-juice company Odwalla, said that the early owners tested procedures themselves to see how long they would take so that the right number of people could be hired to do the work. The owners were typically 70%

more productive than employees. Why? Because most employees are not emotional about their workplace, not emotionally connected to the job. A well done incentive program can bring some of the employee emotional connection back to the workplace.

A good incentive program sets up a series of rewards that employees can achieve for specific performances. Traditionally, they have been most common for salespeople because their performance is easily measured. More recently, they are increasing for other employees as their contributions are being recognized. One of the strongest incentives is personal recognition. A program formalizes that with clear rules that allow people to achieve and be rewarded objectively.

Here is how to create a program to reward internal customer service within your organization.

> ### Reinforce Service
>
> Mutual of Omaha receives over 10,000 bills a day. When a customer called in a panic because Mutual hadn't paid her invoices and she needed the money for medical bills, the claims analyst showed her how to fax another copy and got the check on the way in a hurry. This made the customer grateful and earned the analyst the weekly "Most Valuable Player" award. Employees who win get a sweatshirt and breakfast with the company president. It's considered a big honor by employees and collects great service stories for the company.

1. Review All of the Available Information

- What did your company do in the past to educate employees and encourage them to work together?
- What do you know about the success or failure of the program?
- If you ran the same program today, would the results be different?
- Are there suggestions or complaints that would make a similar program run more smoothly?
- Would management support this effort?

You get what you reward.
—Ken Blanchard

2. Define the Role of the Employees
- Who are the participants?
- What are the limitations, if any, of their ability to solve a problem?
- What is the dollar amount granted to the employees to solve a problem?

3. Set Measurable Objectives or Goals
- Realistic—how realistic is the objective?
- Measurable—is the measurement easy to understand?
- Did the co-workers understand and agree to these objectives?

4. Creative Strategy
- What are we trying to accomplish overall?
- How does this integrate with the overall company objectives?
- How to we get there from here?

5. Review the Objectives and Strategies with Management
- Make sure you have a top management "champion" for the program.
- Make sure the support staff is involved.
- Make sure all department heads understand this program.
- Make sure that you can deliver good products and services. (If the product is poorly made, tastes bad, or is overpriced, employees cannot be proud of what they do.)

6. Determine Tactics
- Communications and promotion—How will this program be launched? How will it be communicated throughout its life?

> If you are trying to change the way you run a company, one of the most visible things you have to change is the way you compensate, reward, and recognize people.
> —Paul Allaire, CEO, Xerox Corp

- administration—Who is in charge? What resources do we have to allocate?
- training and research—Is there any thing that could short circuit this program? How do we train our participants? Have we involved all departments? Did we research what the competition is doing?
- turnaround time—What is a reasonable period of time to accomplish this goal?
- accurate information delivered in a timely manner to participants— progress reports
- trust—keeping promises
- exceeding expectations—delivering more than you promise

7. Follow Through

A properly executed plan sets the tone for continued "internal customer service." Just like the fighter pilot who has the enemy in sight, just before he fires his rocket, he gets "tone." In your programs, you should get "smile" followed by "tones of joy." Remember the program is not successful until the winners say so. If they *feel they are winners,* the sponsoring company will be a winner as well.

Payoffs from Incentives

Benefits of investments in nonsales employee incentive programs:

- Edy's Grand Ice Cream reduced inventory 66%, increased productivity 47%, and increased sales volume 830%.
- Xerox cut new product development time in half.

—From an Ernst & Young study for the U.S. Department of Labor

8. Track the Program

- Assign responsibility.
- Provide reports to each level—participant, managers, and management.
- Fine-tune throughout the program.
- Listen to your participants. Accept any new ideas and try to use them. Re-

spond appropriately and in a timely manner.

- Take what you hear seriously and act fast.
- Create a new program built on the success of the recently completed one.

CONCLUSION

- A dissatisfied employee will not provide exceptional customer service on a long-term basis.
- Internal customer satisfaction is directly related to external customer satisfaction, profits, and growth.
- Internal customer dissatisfaction leads to external customer dissatisfaction and loss of profits.
- Internal customer satisfaction is the key element in creating and keeping long-term customers.

The opportunities for business success have never been more plentiful. Harness the power of your team to dominate your marketplace.

BURST INTO ACTION

I find that the harder I work, the more luck I seem to have.

—Thomas Jefferson

1 Gather input from all employees as to how they see current internal customer service. (In organizational climate studies, you might measure cooperation, support, morale, job satisfaction, and so forth.)

2 Ask employees what they want from their jobs.

3 Calculate your turnover and absenteeism rates and what they cost you. Include costs of "dropping the ball" for customers.

4 Make sure top execs regularly spend some time on the frontline.

5 Find ways to turn your organizational pyramid upside down to emphasize customers and support your staff.

6 Develop a clear message about internal customer service and disseminate it throughout your organization.

7 Develop recognition programs where employees can acknowledge each other for internal service.

8 Develop a larger incentive program where all employees can earn bigger rewards for internal service.

SECTION II
GREAT SERVICE SKILLS

MYSTERY SHOPPERS TELL YOU HOW GOOD
YOUR SERVICE *REALLY* IS
Mark Csordos

TURN COMPLAINTS INTO COMPLIMENTS
Sandra Livermon

ONLINE CUSTOMER SERVICE:
BUILDING A SENSE OF CONNECTION
Jeanette S. Cates

CROSS-CULTURAL CUSTOMER SERVICE FOR
THE 21st CENTURY: ARE YOU PREPARED?
Patricia Zakian Tith

MYSTERY SHOPPERS TELL YOU HOW GOOD YOUR SERVICE *REALLY* IS

Mark Csordos

Mark Csordos
is founder and president of
C&S Mystery Shoppers, Inc.,
a customer service consulting
company. Past and present
clients include firms in the grocery, banking, hotel, and restaurant industries such
as ShopRite, Pizza Hut, and the New Jersey State Lottery.

Mr. Csordos is also an accomplished speaker and teacher. He has been
featured in many national publications including *The New York Times*, *Vogue*,
and *Business Start Ups*. He has appeared on the national radio program
Shopping Smart with Phil Lempert as an expert on service in the supermarket
industry. Mr. Csordos was also selected by *Business News New Jersey* as one
of 1998's "40 under 40"—New Jersey's up-and-coming business people under
the age of 40.

Mr. Csordos is a graduate of Rutgers University with a degree in
communications.

Mark Csordos, C&S Mystery Shoppers, Inc., 77 Milltown Road, East Brunswick, NJ
08816; phone (732) 432-5533; fax (732) 432-5532; e-mail tree871@aol.com.

Chapter 4

MYSTERY SHOPPERS TELL YOU HOW GOOD YOUR SERVICE *REALLY* IS

Mark Csordos

Research is nothing but a state of mind—going out
to look for change instead of waiting for it to come.
—Charles F. Kettering

A new British shopping mall wanted to create a positive and consistent experience by providing great customer service for all shoppers in all stores. A mystery shopping company designed and implemented a program for all of the mall businesses. Banks, restaurants, and retail stores were all appraised by mystery shoppers. Results were used in a recognition and reward program for employees. Now, great customer service is a key differentiator in attracting customers.

WHAT IS MYSTERY SHOPPING?

When I tell people that my company does mystery shopping, it's usually a mystery to them what I'm talking about. What mystery shoppers do is actually very simple. Mystery shoppers pose as customers and formally rate their shopping experiences. They have also been called "mystery customers," "spotters," or "secret shoppers"—and probably a few less pleasant names!

Mystery shoppers are most commonly used in retail organizations, but can be used in any business that has customers. They have been around, formally or informally, since the days of the first department stores.

Besides making in-person visits (or "shops"), mystery shoppers can be used on the phone, online, or any other way a customer might interact with you. They can also be used by you to evaluate your competitors so that you can benchmark yourself against them. The data mystery shoppers provide can be used as an objective way to reward employees, as well as to uncover problems in your operation.

Mystery Shopping by Phone

"Shops" by telephone are similar to in-person shops. A telephone caller evaluates the customer service, friendliness, and product knowledge of the order taker. Other data can be collected such as the number of rings it took for the phone to be answered, whether or not the proper greeting was used, the amount of time the caller remained on hold, and so forth.

For retail stores, phone shops can also be performed in conjunction with in-store shops for the most thorough evaluations.

WHY COMPANIES PAY PEOPLE TO SHOP THEM

The main reason companies use mystery shopping is to give them an *objective* view of their customer service. Let's say I own a store called "Mark's Place."

As the owner of Mark's Place, I can't freely walk around the store and not be noticed by my employees. My mere presence creates unnatural reactions around me. If I do interact with employees, they will more than likely treat me differently than how they treat regular customers. They may either do everything rigidly perfect or they could be more relaxed.

What's Really Happening

When a mystery shopper interacts with an employee, the way the shopper is treated is the way that employee is treating all customers. The shoppers give unbiased accounts of their shopping experiences, both good and bad.

Used over time, mystery shoppers can help identify areas of strength and weakness. For example, let's say Mark's Place has a policy of greeting every customer at the door. When I get the reports back, I can look for trends and figure out how many times the shoppers were actually greeted at the door. Say the shoppers were greeted only 8 out of 20 times at the door. I now know that I have to focus on that area of customer service.

The reports can also be used as a training device to help train new employees to avoid common mistakes made in the past. To reinforce the importance of giving good customer service, I will reward each employee who is mentioned in the reports in an outstanding manner. The rewards don't have to be monetary. Often, just a verbal pat on the back is enough to show the employee that good customer service is noticed and important.

> If you can measure that of which you speak, and can express it by a number, you know something of your subject; but if you cannot measure it, your knowledge is meager and unsatisfactory.
> —William Thomson

DISPELLING MYSTERY SHOPPING MYTHS

Not Spies, Just Ordinary People

I have seen mystery shoppers depicted wearing trench coats and appearing very covert. This has led many to believe that mystery shoppers are used as "spies," and has created a negative image of mystery shopping for some employees.

A good mystery shopping program is one where everyone in the company, from the president to frontline employees, knows it's going on. They know the criteria being evaluated, the objectives of the program, and why it's being done. Usually, the only mystery is the exact time at which it's being done and by whom. The mystery shoppers themselves are ordinary people. They could be a twenty-year-old college student, a mother of two, or a senior citizen.

> ## Praise to Train Employees
>
> While employees are still learning their jobs, the manager needs to catch them doing things right. Praisings that are sincere, specific, timely acknowledgments of progress towards the desired goal reinforce desired performance. The best praisings are done personally, face-to-face with the employee, but written praisings are also effective.
>
> —Ken Blanchard,
> ("The One Minute Manager")

It's true that in the past mystery shopping was sometimes used as a "gotcha" to find out what employees were doing wrong. Today, mystery shopping has become more sophisticated and many companies use a program to find out what employees are doing right. Such positive feedback is crucial to the success of any serious management program.

Who Needs Mystery Shoppers?— I've Got Customers

Store owners and customer service managers sometimes say they don't need to use mystery shopping because, "My customers tell me what they like and don't like." Unfortunately, this is rarely true. As mentioned in Chapter 1, most customers don't return when they're treated with indifference—and few of these unhappy customers bother to complain.

Just think of your own experiences. Every time you like or dislike something at a store, do you tell the manager? Of course not. Think of some very bad customer service you have received. Did you find out who the owner of that establishment was and then call or send them a letter? Probably not. We're all just too busy.

You *may* complain to the manager on duty, but unless you raise a stink, your complaint probably won't go any higher. (Research shows that only about 5%–10% of complaints get passed on to top management.)

If you're like most people, you'll simply take your business elsewhere next time and complain about your experience to your friends and family. Studies show that 96% of dissatisfied customers never complain, they just never return. When you add that to the few of complaints that get passed up to the top, perhaps only four complaints in 1,000 get passed along to top management.

Mystery Shopping at Banks

Like retailers, banks use mystery shoppers to determine if service promises are being met. Additionally, many banks use mystery shopper feedback to assess how comfortable employees feel with new products. If a new product isn't being mentioned, more training is given to increase employees' product knowledge.

It's Not Just for Retail Companies

Every company has customers. Good service isn't limited to retail businesses. Business-to-business service is also "shoppable." The ABC Company orders a product from XYZ, Inc. The order is three days late and arrives damaged. ABC calls to complain and the XYZ employee on the phone is rude or disinterested. What is the ABC Company going to do? They're going to use a different company next time. XYZ, Inc. would benefit from telephone "shops."

THE MYSTERY SHOPPING PROCESS

Now, let's go step by step through the mystery shopping process, from deciding on your goals to getting the results and implementing customer service improvements. We'll again use Mark's Place to illustrate the process.

Step 1: Deciding What You Want from the Program

Let's assume that you and I are co-owners of Mark's Place and we'd like to use mystery shopping to improve our customer service. Where do we start?

First, we need to discuss the objectives of the program. For it to succeed, we need to be clear on what we want the program to accomplish. We'll discuss and answer the questions in the box at the right before we move ahead.

Let's say we have decided to do one mystery shop every week. We will introduce the program at our next managers' meeting. We will explain that the goal is to raise our level of customer service by doing more of what we do right and correcting our problem areas.

The reports will give us an objective way to evaluate those areas. We will also explain that the reports aren't going to be used to fire employees. Employees who do not perform up to par will be spoken to, and retrained if necessary. We will reward employees who perform well, first with a verbal acknowledgment and, later, for those employees who distinguish themselves over several reports, with a gift certificate to a local restaurant or movie theater.

> ### Define Your Objectives
>
> Answer these questions before you implement a mystery shopping program:
> - What are your long-term goals with this customer service program?
> - How will you introduce the program to employees? How will you pick the criteria to be evaluated?
> - How will you present the reports, both good and bad, to your employees?
> - What are you trying to accomplish with the reports? How often will you do the shops?
> - What happens when you accomplish your goals?

When we accomplish our goal of averaging a score of 90 each week for six months, we will reevaluate the program and look for new ways to improve our customer service.

Managers then discuss the program with their employees. It's actually a good—but underutilized—idea to get your employees involved in the process early. Employees also often enjoy shopping your competitors for ideas of behaviors and attributes to evaluate in your mystery shopping program. They will have unique insights about customer interactions. And, if they help create the forms they are rated and rewarded on, they will be less suspicious of the process.

Step 2: Establishing the Criteria That Will Be Evaluated

Most good mystery shopping companies will already have forms developed that meet many businesses' needs. But let's say we want to develop our own criteria. One of the best ways to do this is to go shop at a close competitor. It's easier to be objective about your competitor than it is your own business, and you will also go unnoticed.

Going on a sample shop. We'll say Mark's Place is a supermarket for this example, but the process would be no different for any other retailer or service business.

We arrive at our competitor, Jen's Market. What is the first thing we notice as we drive up? The parking lot and the front of the building. That will be our first question. Were the lot and sidewalk clean and free of debris? Were shopping carts

neatly lined up and available for customers? If we go at night, was there adequate lighting?

We then walk through the vestibule. That will be our second question. Was the vestibule clean? Were there circulars available? We then walk over to the courtesy counter. We wait in line thirty seconds and ask in what aisle we could find the peanut butter. Jane smiles and tells us it's down aisle three, on the left-hand side about halfway down.

What would we like to know about when our customers go to our courtesy desk? Was the clerk wearing a name badge? Yes. Who waited on the shopper? In this case, Jane. How long did the shopper wait in line? Thirty seconds. Was the clerk prompt, friendly, and helpful? Yes, she smiled and told us right where the product would be. So those would be our questions for the courtesy counter.

We would walk through the other departments the same way. What does a customer want when they shop the meat department? They want the meat to be fresh. They want a large variety of products to choose from. They want the shelves to be clean. They want signs displayed showing prices of the items. We would go around the store and ask ourselves these questions for each department. By the time we leave the store, we would have most of our form developed.

Excerpt of a Sample Mystery Shopper Scoring Sheet

STORE __Jen's Market__

DATE __7/24__   SHOPPER __DP__

WAS THE PARKING LOT CLEAN? (YES) NO

TIME ENTERED STORE __11:48__

TIME EXITED STORE __12:12__

TIME SPENT WAITING FOR EMPLOYEE ASSISTANCE __30 secs__ .

WHEN ASKING FOR HELP IN LOCATING AN ITEM, DID THE EMPLOYEE:

✓ MAKE EYE CONTACT AND SMILE

✓ DIRECT YOU TO THE CORRECT AISLE

___ ESCORT YOU TO LOCATION

EMPLOYEE NAME __Jane__

NUMBER OF CUSTOMERS IN LONGEST CHECKOUT LINE __4__

NUMBER OF CHECKOUT LANES OPEN __2__

You may want to add some of your company's criteria that the customer wouldn't know about. For example, you may want each cashier to use a particular greeting. You may want your customers greeted as they enter the store. The customer wouldn't know about either of these, but they're part of your criteria and can be included in the form.

Good and Bad Service Received by Actual Mystery Shoppers

GOOD

- Employees who accommodate customers' slightly unusual requests. For example, "Can I return an item from Store A to Store B?" [This costs relatively little money, but creates a lot of goodwill.]
- Deli employees who offer tastes of products without being asked.
- If a customer is looking for an out-of-stock item, they are given a substitution for a comparable item instead of a rain check or being told, "Sorry, we're out."
- Stores that allow customers to use competitors' coupons or rain checks to prevent customers from shopping at that store.

BAD

- Employees who complain about how they hate to work there while they are waiting on customers. [This is a frequent experience.]
- Employees who bad-mouth their boss or, worse, other customers, while waiting on customers.
- In supermarkets, a common response asking if there is any more of an item is, "If it's not on the shelf, we don't have it."
- A shopper observed two employees throwing eggs at each other down one of the aisles. A customer was splashed with some yolk.

Scoring yourself. If you choose, you can assign a point value to each question. You will have to decide how to weight each question. For example, which is more important, the cashier not asking for coupons or the ground meat not being fresh? Using a point system also allows you to track progress over time. You can compare the current month's report to six months prior and see if you are making improvements. Just be careful not to get too caught up in the score. Sometimes, it's easy to focus so much on the score that you may not see what the score means or the comments that are in the report.

Another option would be to do a narrative report. In this type of report, the shoppers describe their experiences detail by detail. You may also choose to do a combination of both. In the end, choose the one that best fits your needs.

Step 3: Picking the Right Mystery Shopping Company

As in all industries, all mystery shopping companies are not equal. You would not call the lawyer who handled your house closing to represent you in a criminal case. For instance, my company does not do integrity shops. Those are shops where the shoppers are checking for employee theft. This is a speciality. If a shopper visits a location and accuses an employee of theft, they're potentially opening themselves up to a lawsuit.

Some companies are regional or specialize in certain fields such as banking or real estate. It's important to pick a company that is right for you. The first question you should ask is if the prospective company specializes in mystery shopping. Some companies offer many services and mystery shopping is one of them. Next, you should ask if they cover the area where you are located. Some companies are regional and only shop in a particular state or region.

Customization and change. An important question is if they customize their forms. You will want a form that suits your company's needs exactly and is not just a cookie cutter form for your industry. Some companies will charge a fee to design a form, so you may wish to develop one yourself. Another important issue to find out is if you can change the program over time. If you want to make minor changes, it should not be a problem and it shouldn't cost you anything.

Check *their* customer service. Ask the mystery shopper company for references and check *their* customer service. I am amazed at how many people have told me that they used XYZ Mystery Shopping company and that XYZ didn't return phone calls, did sloppy work, didn't proofread the reports, and so forth. If their customer service isn't good, how can they help you improve yours?

Checklist for Hiring a Mystery Shopping Company

- Has the company worked with other businesses with similar needs as yours?
- Does the company specialize in mystery shopping?
- Will the company customize its forms to fit your specific needs? If so, is there a charge for this?
- Do the company's current customers give it a good rating? (Are reports clear and received on time?)
- Will the company describe its criteria for hiring shoppers?
- Does the company guarantee its work?

Also ask where the companies get their shoppers. Our office has received letters from people who want to be mystery shoppers that would make a third-grade teacher cry over their physical and grammatical sloppiness, yet they tell us they have worked as mystery shoppers for other companies.

Make sure you know how the mystery shopping company hires its shoppers.

A good mystery shopping company will have met most of their shoppers. Be careful of the companies that just pick their shoppers from a database and send them assignments sight unseen. They may have a hard time maintaining consistent quality.

It's okay to ask a company to send a sample of what they do, but don't expect them to send you your competitor's report. You'll probably just get a generic sample. You should also find out if you're required to sign a contract for a minimum length of time or number of shops.

Of course, the next question you will ask is about price. The price could vary widely depending on the amount of time it takes to do the shops, how involved the shop is, how many locations are being shopped, and whether or not the shoppers have to make purchases during the visit. Costs can vary widely between mystery shopping companies.

Ask if the company guarantees its work. A good company should say that if you're not satisfied with the reports, you won't have to pay for them. It's important to remember that in this case, you're the customer and they'll have to meet your needs.

Step 4: Introducing the Program to Your Employees

If you haven't involved your employees from the beginning, now is the time to introduce the shopping to your employees. Some companies decide not to tell their employees about the mystery shopping, but it's always better when they're a part of the process. Employees can't correct mistakes if they don't know the specific behaviors you want performed. You may choose to notify your employees by a memo, in the newsletter, or at the managers' meeting.

Let's go back to our fictional Mark's Place. Remember, we already introduced the idea to our managers. Now we will tell our managers that we will be using mystery shoppers to improve our customer service and give us an edge on our competition. There will probably be some reluctance at first because of the myths described earlier in the chapter.

Employee concerns. All concerns should be immediately addressed. We will show the managers the form we developed and ask them for their input. If the mystery shopping company has literature, we will hand that out, too. You want to make your employees as comfortable with the program (and the company that will be performing the shops) as possible. If the employees don't have faith in the company or the program, you'll be wasting your money. Everyone needs to believe in the program and its goals in order for it to be successful.

> ## Motivational Aspects of Mystery Shoppers
>
> Market Trends Research Company reports that financial institutions have seen dramatic changes in service levels by simply letting the branch staff know that the mystery shopper was coming!
>
> In reality, every customer is performing an evaluation. But the evaluation—good or bad—is generally not shared with either the company or the individual. When employees know a customer might be turning in a written evaluation of their performance, it's only natural that they try harder.

We will describe to them what is going to be done with the reports and how the employees who are "shopped" will be handled. It's important to reiterate that the goal of the program is to improve customer service, thereby improving the company's competitive position—and even job security—and not to catch employees doing something wrong.

Step 5: What to Do with the Reports Now that You Have Them

The moment of truth. Your first report is coming over the fax. Two words of warning: BE PREPARED. Sometimes businesses are amazed at the service level (or lack of) they offer their customers when they read the first couple of reports. At least now, though, you will have a way to track your service and improve your weak areas. And if the reports are good, you're ahead of the game.

Let's take a look at Mark's Place. We look over our first report and the average score is 85. In high school that was a "B" so the report isn't too bad.

Over time you will find out what your store's scoring average should be. You'll need about 10–20 reports to establish your true average score. After that, you can look at scoring changes as improvements or declines in your customer service. I also make sure I look at the comments that accompany each section and not just the score. I now decide that the report should be forwarded to the store manager and other appropriate personnel. We will decide what steps should be taken and which employees need to be retrained, if any.

Report Card

	Goal	Score
Cleanliness	95	90
Initial Greeting	95	85
Overall friendliness	85	80
Helpfulness of employees	85	82
Merchandise in stock	95	85
Thanking customers for their business	100	88

Constructive Feedback

It's important to discuss the report and why things happened and not just grill employees. I would discuss what was good and what we will need to focus on and improve. Each manager will then sit down with their employees who were shopped and discuss their performance. This is also a good opportunity to reinforce your customer service philosophy.

For example, on the report for Mark's Place, the comment on the deli says that Angela was very helpful and friendly when assisting the shopper. As the manager, I would thank her for doing a good job and tell her to keep it up. This would give me a good chance to reinforce the importance of customer service to our company and give her a pat on the back.

Unfortunately, the cashier section wasn't as positive. According to the report, the cashier did not greet the shopper and did not do most of the things we want our cashiers to do. I would also sit with this cashier and discuss her performance. I would remain positive and explain that providing great customer service is what keeps our customers coming back. I would discuss with her the front-end policies (the specific behaviors we want our cashiers to do) and make sure she understood them. I would also emphasize that in the future this kind of report would be unacceptable.

Share shopper results. I would post the overall shop scores by the time clock so everyone would be aware of our performance, but I think it's best to meet with individual employees in private. This way, the employee isn't put "on the spot" discussing their performance. It's important to keep the program positive but still stress that sub-par performances are not acceptable.

Step 6: Using the Reports Over Time

If you have averaged an 80 for six months, make it your goal to reach 85. Always keep revising your goals upward.

Over time, you can also use the report to look at both good

STAFF ANNOUNCEMENT

Mystery shopping score for the month of July   84

This is a 2-point increase over last week. We're scoring high on cleanliness and overall friendliness. Congratulations! Areas we need to concentrate on are keeping advertised specials on the shelves and greeting customers as they enter the store.

Keep up the good work. Let's see if we can get up to an 85 next month.

and bad trends that are developing. For example, if your employees have failed to perform Item #3 (for example, thanking customers for their business) in 40 out of 50 reports, you have a training issue to deal with rather than poor individual performance.

As the program progresses, you may also want to change the form you are using to one that is more challenging and requires employees to perform even better. In time, mystery phone shops or mystery delivery service shops (if applicable) can be added in conjunction with in-person shops.

Customer Care

It's so important to CARE about your customers because

C ustomers
A lways
R emember
E verything

WITHOUT FEEDBACK, IT'S HARD TO IMPROVE

Remember, ALL COMPANIES already have mystery shoppers, but most of them never give you feedback. They're your customers. Every customer who deals with you is making his or her own mental ratings of your service. Ultimately, mystery shopping is a tool to deliver better service to your customers. That's really what it's all about, isn't it?

BURST INTO ACTION

Without ambition one starts nothing. Without work one finishes nothing.

—Ralph Waldo Emerson

1 Set up a schedule to shop your competitors regularly. Encourage your employees to do so also. Use your findings to benchmark your business.

2 Establish specific customer service criteria—for example, greet customer within 10 seconds, answer phone by second ring, automatically offer a rain check for out-of-stock items, use customer's name when possible.

3 List five ways you could use data from a mystery shopper program.

4 Call several mystery shopper services. Evaluate their services to find the one or two that best fit your needs. Then check their references.

5 Discuss mystery shopper programs with your staff. Solicit their input on criteria and procedures. Tell them how the data will be used.

6 Decide how to discuss data with individual employees. Remember, reprimands should always be private; praisings can be public.

7 Consider use of a reward program for employees who give good service (name and photo on plaque in store, gift certificates to restaurants, name in company newsletter, and so forth). (See also Chapter 3.)

8 If you are part of a shopping center or other multi-business complex, talk with other owners and center management to see if coordinating an overall mystery shopper program is feasible and desirable.

TURN COMPLAINTS INTO COMPLIMENTS

Sandra Livermon

Sandra Livermon
is a professional speaker,
trainer, and consultant, as well
as an award-winning building
contractor. Her work focuses on three areas: people skills, communication, and
personal development; customer service and sales; and teamwork and leadership development. Her clients include Hardees, Sprint, NationsBank, National
Association of Home Builders, Mutual of Omaha, and General Motors.

In her seminars, workshops, and keynote speeches, she incorporates "real
world" lessons learned from her 24 years of owning and operating her own
construction company. Her presentations are unique in the industry. Using her
experiences and exceptional storytelling abilities, she inspires, motivates, and
informs her audiences. Those who know her say Ms. Livermon's greatest talent
is finding the talent of those around her and inspiring them to use it.

She has been on the covers of *Builder/Architect* and *Today's Changing
Woman* magazines, and featured in *Interviews and Reviews* magazine. She has
done many radio and television interviews and recently filmed a ten-part television editorial. Ms. Livermon also writes a column in *Horizons* magazine.

Ms. Livermon has a degree in economics. She is married with two children.

Sandra Livermon, P.O. Box 83345, Rocky Mount, NC 27804; phone (252) 443–
0541, (800) 365-7071; fax (252) 443-1136; e-mail sandi@sandisays.com;
www.sandisays.com.

Chapter 5

TURN COMPLAINTS INTO COMPLIMENTS

Sandra Livermon

It is time for all organizations to think of complaint handling as a strategic tool . . . rather than as a nuisance or cost.

—Janelle Barlow and Claus Møller, *A Complaint Is a Gift*

H andling complaints is the most misunderstood, overlooked, and undervalued part of customer service. Yet it is a skill that can be easily developed through awareness, commitment, and training.

Developing complaint-resolution skills is a partnership. Companies must be committed to training and empowering their workforces. Just as importantly, the *entire* workforce must commit to implementing these skills. The ability and willingness to satisfy complaints is not only vital to the longevity and success of an organization but is a highly prized, marketable skill for the individual. From frontline employee to CEO, the ability and willingness to turn customer complaints into compliments is more precious than gold. If you have this skill, you will always be in demand and valued in the workplace.

Studies have shown that when a complaint is handled quickly and satisfactorily, the customer not only remains a customer but actually is more loyal than ever—even more than customers who never had a complaint. In fact, 7 of 10 do business with the person or company again IF the complaint is resolved in their favor—and 95% return if you resolve the problem on the spot!

Repeat Business from Dissatisfied Customers

70%	95%
Complaint resolved favorably	Complaint resolved on the spot

Why is that? People do not expect perfection. They do, however, expect their needs to be met and their expectations realized whenever they are investing in your product or service.

Complaints arise in many different situations. They are sometimes expressed, but more frequently they are not expressed. Let's look at two examples before I discuss the major ways to train employees to satisfy complaints.

When You're in the Wrong

THE SITUATION: Bud had an armful of dry cleaning to pick up and just as much to leave. The counter person was embarrassed to show Bud one of his shirts. It looked like it had been through a shredder!

THE COMPLAINT: A usable shirt was ruined.

The faster you can respond to a customer's problem, the more likely it is that the customer will not even remember that there was a problem. The slower you are in responding, the more likely it is that the problem will become significant.
—Michael E. Cafferky,
Let Your Customers Do the Talking

THE SOLUTION: After inspecting the shirt, the owner asked Bud what it would take to satisfy him. Since the shirt wasn't new, Bud suggested a $20 credit. The owner immediately pulled the tickets from the remaining garments to be picked up. The total was $63.60. He tore the tickets in half, helped Bud take the clothing to his car, apologized once more and asked him to return.

THE RESULT: Bud has been a loyal customer for the past 12 years.

When there is a breakdown at any point in the service process, complaints *may* result. It is important to note that only 4% of dissatisfied customers complain to you or the company.

Sound great? No. It's terrible! You need complaints. Instead, individuals air their complaints to *anyone else* who will listen, or silently take their business elsewhere. This underscores the need to be trained and alert to interpret the *unspoken signs* of discontent. Only then can you explore the problem and take action to resolve the customer's concerns.

Complaints Are Hidden

It is estimated that of the unhappy customers who do complain, only 5%–10% of complaints reach top management. Most talk to front-line people such as the sales force or customer service reps. This means that top management is getting a distorted view of the number of complaints.

Internal Customers

Complaints from employees—internal customers—are the best barometer for measuring the level of buy-in by employees to the culture of the company.

THE SITUATION: A large manufacturing company's warehouse was filling to capacity. More product was on hand than ever before. There was a growing concern among employees that something was wrong. *Never* had so much merchandise been stockpiled.

Rumors were rampant. Employees began updating their resumes and looking for new jobs. It was generally felt that either the company was going to be bought out or orders were declining to such a point that the company was going under.

THE COMPLAINT: Employees resented not being kept informed of what was happening. There were many unanswered questions. No one knew what to expect, but no formal "complaint" was ever forthcoming.

Hold a Company Complaint Session

What better way to show that complaints are valued than to run a company complaint session? Organize an informal forum or roundtable. Ideally, it should be facilitated by an outside person or by another neutral party so employees won't feel threatened if they reveal too much. Often, this can be the start of important initiatives and help make workers at all levels feel more a part of the company.

THE SOLUTION: The company was actually enjoying their greatest period of prosperity. Orders were coming in so quickly that the stockpile was an effort to meet external customers demands. An intensive campaign was launched to communicate to the entire workforce the positive, rather than negative, direction of the company.

THE RESULT: New excitement and enthusiasm. Employees now feel part of the new success.

THE VALUE OF COMPLAINTS

Complaints from external customers are your best chance to dramatically increase customer satisfaction. Complaints from *any* source are educational moments. They must not be taken lightly or disregarded. Your goal is to master the art of dealing with complaints successfully and to use complaints as a barometer for judging and improv-

Prerequisites for Developing Complaint Resolution Skill

1. **Decide.** It is difficult to develop the skill of turning complaints into compliments if you have not made a philosophical decision to do so.

2. **Have a plan**—but be spontaneous. Think out possible responses and what you want to communicate. Be spontaneous by personalizing the options you've planned to suit the needs of each customer.

3. **Paint a picture in your head.** Too often employees can't visualize having the skill and the confidence to take control of a negative situation and turn it into a positive experience for everyone. The trick is to take mental control. See the situation being resolved successfully and favorably for EVERYONE.

4. **Be accessible and approachable.** Before any positive steps can be made to turn the complaint into a compliment, you must be accessible to the person with the complaint. Customers are intuitive. They must feel it is worth their time and effort to make their complaints known.

ing performance. Complaints give a clear and realistic picture of "where you stand."

Why are soliciting and handling complaints the weakest links in customer service?

1. There is little or no emphasis placed on training employees to handle the inevitable reality that complaints *will* arise. What to do with complaints and how to do it are given minimum attention by most training programs. Poor training adds to people's stress and lack of confidence in handling complaints. The result is that individuals are left to deal with both the complaints and their discomfort by themselves.

2. Because individuals feel insecure or uncomfortable handling complaints, they often try to ignore the problem. This only compounds the situation and adds to the customer's frustration. Correcting the problem can be one of the most rewarding parts of customer service. Successful complaint resolution delights the customer. You become the hero, not the villain.

3. More important than the successful resolution of the 4% of voiced complaints is the resolution of the 96% of unvoiced complaints. Employees fail to ask identifying questions. Everyone from frontline through management is often oblivious to signals of customer discontent.

External *and* Internal Complaints

When you misunderstand or ignore complaints, they lose their "asset value."

THE SITUATION: A major bank was adding a large number of new services and products. They were doing extensive advertising to acquaint the public with their new program.

THE COMPLAINT: Customers would call to get additional information or sign up for a new service or product and employees would know *little or nothing* about them. Employees complained they felt embarrassed and incompetent when put on the spot. They had been given *no* information or training except perhaps seeing the local advertisements.

To date there has been no attempt by the bank to "find out" why the programs are not being embraced by the public or why there is so much resistance by the employees to "selling" the new services. No one is available or willing to listen or explain. After repeated complaints from customers and employees were continuously ignored, neither group now bothers to make their complaints known.

THE SOLUTION: None has been suggested, attempted, or the need even acknowledged.

THE RESULT: Customers *and* employees are frustrated. Customers are going elsewhere. Employees feel added pressure to "sell" a service they know nothing about and their stress level is increasing. Employees criticize the company in public.

Remember only 4% of dissatisfied customers complain. That does not mean 96% are happy. They have made a decision based on the signals they are receiving. "No one cares—what good will it do?"

> An individual without information cannot take responsibility; an individual who is given information cannot help but take responsibility.
> —Jan Carlzon, *Moments of Truth*

7 STEPS FOR TURNING COMPLAINTS INTO COMPLIMENTS

Employees who are trained to use these seven steps skillfully and naturally will be more confident and more willing to handle complaints. People who are at ease with their abilities are more likely to be pleasant, relaxed and have a sense of humor when dealing with others.

Making It Easier for Customers to Complain

Canadian Tire retail outlets have a video booth in the center of their stores to record customer complaints. Merely having their complaints recorded probably calms down some customers and also gives the company valuable information.

Step 1: Be Appreciative and Empathic

A. Thank them first thing! Let the customer know that you appreciate them taking the time and effort to bring their complaint to your attention. It is very difficult to maintain a high degree of rage and hostility in the face of someone's *sincere* appreciation. It is vitally important to truly empathize with your customer. Be supportive and clearly communicate your appreciation for being given the opportunity to "make it right."

B. Be calm. Stay under control. Finding acceptable solutions requires clear thinking and sound judgment. Individuals do not make their best decisions and are not creative problem-solvers when they are agitated, angry, or defensive. Being calm and in control of your emotions is a show of strength. It will open the lines of communication. Someone on the defensive is a poor communicator. Statements made in haste and in the heat of the moment are never beneficial. Focus on the event or action that needs to be corrected. Never accuse or verbally attack the individual. Just as importantly, don't take the complaint personally. *Focus on the problem, not the personality.*

Speak when you are angry, and you will make the best speech you'll ever regret.

—Ambrose Bierce

C. Make it easy. Remember, there are few "*only's.*" Customers have an endless choice of goods and services from which to chose. Why should customers waste their time, effort and dollars where they are not appreciated? If you hide and customers must seek, they will seek someone else to listen—and somewhere else to spend their money! Make it easy for customers to share their complaints with you.

D. Respond enthusiastically. Be happy and generous in dealing with complaints. Enthusiasm is contagious. Let the customer see and experience your eagerness and enthusiasm to satisfy them. Make dealing with their complaint an experience to be remembered in a *positive* way.

You can't convince anyone that you are pleased to have this opportunity if your attitude is *negative.* Every individual has complete control over his or her attitude and level of enthusiasm. Whatever individuals really *want* to do, they can find the energy and enthusiasm to do it. Your enthusiasm reflects your attitude, level of caring, and degree of commitment. *It sends a clearer message than any words.*

Enthusiasm Leader

The San Francisco Chronicle reports that Lee Lucas, president of several Saturn dealerships in California and Hawaii, has created a staff position called the "customer enthusiasm representative." It is this person's job to contact and stay in touch with customers after the sale, to talk about the sales experience and to find out any problems they might be having.

Step 2: Acknowledge Their Feelings

People who are upset and have a complaint want someone to acknowledge their distress, distrust, and other feelings. Complaints are *real* and *personal.* There are no *small* complaints. Individuals react differently and perceive every situation differently. What is extremely upsetting to one may go unnoticed by another. Acknowledge their feelings (for example, "I can see you are very frustrated"). This tells the individual you are paying attention and are sensitive to what they are feeling at the moment.

Don't tell customers you know how they feel. You probably don't. Everyone's frame of reference is different. Let each individual own and express *their* feelings.

Give people adequate time to vent their feelings. Don't rush to cut them off or even interrupt to offer a solution. Once they have expressed their feelings, they are much more open to working *with you* to resolve the complaint.

Confirm what you have heard. This validates their feelings and lets them know you understand. The customer must feel that you are empathic, not patronizing. This creates a bond between you and the customer. It establishes the foundation for working together.

The customer, first and foremost, must feel you care. This is especially critical for all frontline employees. These are the individuals who can resolve more customer complaints than managers ever will. The game of customer satisfaction and turning complaints into compliments must be won with the players on the field—the front line.

> ## Why Don't Unhappy Customers Complain?
>
> One reason so few unhappy customers complain is that in order to complain, they have to handle confrontations that they fear will produce more stress than their current dissatisfaction. Most decide to take the path of least stress and not complain.
>
> By the time customers call you or walk in your store to complain, many are "psyched up" and prepared for battle.

Step 3: Give the Customer a *"Person"* to Talk To

A. A complaint tends to mushroom and grow to giant proportions when the customer tries in vain to find *someone*. Customers think "if no one in the company cares enough to take my call, how can they possibly care enough to do something about my problem?" Companies and employees must realize the importance of accessibility. Make it easy for your customers to tell you what they are thinking.

B. Accept responsibility. It is the role of management to train and empower *everyone* in the organization to accept complaints and give them the authority to take action. That is not to say that anyone can solve everything. It does mean that everyone must be free to "do something." A shrug and mumbling "you can call the manager if you want" is not taking responsibility. It is not the customer's responsibility to embark on a search-and-find expedition. Employees, from the front line to the front office, must know when and where to get the answers they need to help the customer *now*.

C. Do it now. Respond immediately. Complaints should never be put on hold. It is important for customers to see that you attach a real sense of urgency to their distress. Small problems magnify quickly when they are ignored. *Make addressing any and every complaint a top priority*. Be persistent in your efforts. The customer *will* notice.

D. There is NO customer service department. How often have you had a complaint, an inquiry or problem, and been told by every employee you approached that the "customer service department is over there." Usually this department is hidden away. This reinforces the customer's belief that no one cares. Customer service is *everyone's* job and therefore dealing with complaints is also everyone's job. Making the customers happy, meeting their needs and resolving their complaints means you must remain up-front, personal, and accessible.

Respond Fast to Problems

In one study, Micron Technology had more complaints about their computers than other companies, but fixed them so promptly and cheerfully that 88% of customers said they'd buy again from them. And customers who had a problem were more likely to buy again than those who didn't.

—*Executive Edge* newsletter

Step 4: Be Honest and Sincere

Nothing is more insulting and maddening than to feel someone is trying to con you, or say anything to get you out of the office or off the phone. If the customer doubts your sincerity, the situation only gets worse. The following steps will help you demonstrate your sincere interest and concern:

A. Always apologize. "I apologize for the problem. I am sorry this happened. Let's see what I can do." Take the complaint seriously. It is a *big* deal to your customer. Always acknowledge this as a real problem and *make no excuses*. Passing the buck is a waste of time and destroys your credibility.

B. Give the person your *undivided* attention. Customers must *know* that their complaints are, at that moment, your *top* priority. To change your focus by answering the telephone, stopping to talk to someone, or any other activity, destroys your credibility for sincerely wanting to "make it right." Listen, listen, listen. If customers feel they cannot rely on you to even listen to their complaints, there will be no foundation of trust. The customers must feel you sincerely desire to resolve their complaints.

C. Maintain eye contact, smile, and keep your tone of voice pleasant and nonconfrontational. This will defuse hostilities and relieve tension. Studies have shown that, in conflict situations, people can react more to how you present yourself than to what you say. Remember, customers have been thinking about their complaints. Their emotions are already aroused.

D. Don't keep score. If someone has a complaint, it is the responsibility of the *first* person they encounter to relieve the customer of the burden of that complaint. Customers won't believe you when you say you want to help if they see you trying to *"pass them off"* to someone else. Playing internal games of placing blame is distracting and creates tension among employees. Customers can and will sense this tension.

Step 5: Solicit Solutions

THE SITUATION: Long lines and slow service at the drive-through window of a major fast food restaurant.

THE COMPLAINT: Wasted time and no one seemed to care.

THE SOLUTION: The restaurant asked their customers for suggestions. From customer input, a plan was made and implemented. Now any time more than three cars are in line, two employees go outside, rain or shine, and take over the ordering and payment process. Orders are taken by one person and the second employee takes payment and makes change. When customers reach the drive-through window, they have only to pick up their orders.

RESULT: Often customers *never* have to come to a complete stop. They literally "roll right on through."

A. Ask open-ended questions and the customer will talk to you. This is vital. It is difficult to resolve a problem, re-establish a relationship and build on that relationship if there is no dialogue. As the customer talks, you gain insight into what he or she *really* feels. Ask questions like: "what would make you feel better about this?" "What would you like to see happen?" *Don't guess at the solution to the problem. You'll probably be wrong.* It is important to constantly remind yourself that every customer is a unique individual. There are no generic solutions. There are no

Consumers are statistics. Customers are people.
—Stanley Marcus, Neiman-Marcus

generic complaints. People do not appreciate being second guessed. Ask for solutions.

B. Establish a partnership. If the customer has a problem, the company *and* every employee have a problem. We know that it takes at least six times more effort to attract a new customer (and employee) than to keep them. If a company is losing its customer base because complaints are handled poorly, the company will have serious long-term survival problems. It is also to the employees' benefit that customers be retained. Every person in the workforce, every frontline employee MUST understand that it is in *their best interest* for the company to be successful. They must make the connection between the company's prosperity and their own opportunities for advancement and enrichment. The key is to establish a "we're in this together" atmosphere between the company, the employee, and the customer. The customer must feel you are all working to solve *his or her problem.*

Don't Take the Monkey

William Oncken, Jr., in *Managing Management Time,* pointed out that employees will delegate TO their bosses by asking questions about how to solve problems. Don't take the monkey on your back. Make employees come to you with suggested solutions.

Internal complaints demand the same degree of prompt, caring, and satisfactory resolution as external complaints. It is difficult for employees to focus and care about the needs of the customer if there are unresolved conflicts, issues, and complaints raging within. For customers to get the undivided attention they deserve, all internal complaints must be answered and resolved quickly. Internal distractions are deadly to overall customer service and satisfaction.

Step 6: Say What You'll Do and Do What You Say

THE SITUATION: Katherine was leaving for Europe. Her new credit card had not arrived. Reiterating their national TV promise, she was told that the card would be waiting at her first destination.

THE COMPLAINT: Not only did the card not arrive as promised, but she received the same promise in city after city. Hours of her trip were wasted on the telephone, locating local offices, and waiting for promised delivery. When she spoke with the U.S. home office (when she could get more than a recorded message), her inquiries were handled by a different person who gave a new promise each time.

THE SOLUTION: Totally unsatisfactory.

THE RESULT: The card was delivered four days before the trip was complete—seven weeks late. She had $1100 in telephone bills and no one ever offered an explanation or apology. Now a successful business women, she has changed to another credit card company.

A. Be realistic. Make *only* the promises you can keep *and then keep them.* Be realistic about the time frames.

B. Keep the customer informed every step of the way. If it is a question of getting information or material from another source, let the customer know what must be done, the process

From the Mouths of Customers. . .

Here are a few stories of potential customer disasters that were turned into positive experiences.

No room at the inn. An editor arrived at a hotel to the news that they did not have her reserved room. However, the hotel offered her a free room at their sister property across the street, and a free dinner and breakfast from the hotel restaurant. The editor says, "I felt well taken care of, and I'll call them again the next time I'm going to be there."

Left behind. A consultant was catching the last flight out of Newark to San Francisco. The flight was delayed and he went to United's Red Carpet Club. The attendant promised to notify him when it was time to board. When he looked up, his plane had departed! The attendant gave him a voucher for a cab to Kennedy Airport where he could catch a later flight. There, a United employee met him at the curb, apologized, told him he was a valued customer, and escorted him to his plane. The consultant says that he is more loyal to United now than before the incident: "No reward was involved. It was simply an acknowledgment of my worth to the company . . ."

and the time involved. People are much more agreeable, patient, and tolerant when they know what to expect. Remember you want the customer to feel like you are partnering with them to resolve their complaint.

C. Be reliable. Complaints are defining moments in your and the company's relationship with your customer. Do not underestimate their importance. Reliability is the foundation of trust and a demonstration of integrity. Walk your talk.

> The economics of complaint handling will almost always work out to your benefit, as long as you pay attention to resolving one problem at a time, in a collaborative fashion, with each individual complaining customer.
> —Don Peppers and Martha Rogers, *The One to One Future*

Step 7: Follow Up

THE SITUATION: I was completing a very large house for a widow. She was worried about managing the house alone and how she would get minor upkeep duties done.

THE COMPLAINT: She thought that once we had finished the actual construction, and turned the house over to her, she would be unable to get anyone back to do "small jobs." She was convinced everyone would be too busy to bother.

THE SOLUTION: After she moved in, I gave her the names and numbers of all the subcontractors who had done work on her house. She also got a list of everyone in my office and how they could be contacted whenever she needed *anything.* Then once a week, we called *her* to see if everything was all right. In the weeks that followed, we installed can openers, pegged a knot hole that she thought was a bug, and did other "little things."

THE RESULT: The home owner never felt abandoned. It made a *big* difference. She has been a long-time advocate for us as she shares her praise with others.

A. The process of resolving a complaint is not complete when customers walk out of the building or hang up the telephone. Show that you remember. Call, send a note, or remember them on their next visits. Let customers know that you have valued and acted on their complaints as a stepping stone to improvement. Now take it one step further. Ask again, "*are you R-E-A-L-L-Y satisfied?*"

B. Ask for their continued business. It is important that customers know they are still wanted. Remember, a complaint does *not* make a customer a "problem customer." The customer is not the problem. Once a complaint is resolved, the customer will tell five people that you did so satisfactorily. The customer WILL come back . . . and probably bring their friends!

CONCLUSION

These seven steps apply to internal and external customers with equal importance. The consequences of losing your customer base is obvious. Your job, your product, and your company cannot survive if customer erosion is allowed to happen.

Unresolved complaints *within* the workplace are just as costly and damaging. Companies are often baffled by low morale, turnover, absenteeism, failure to work together, and declining productivity. Well meaning companies spend vast amounts of time and money on incentive plans, programs, and slogans, yet forget to listen to the heartbeats of their organizations—how people "feel." Training everyone in an organization to listen for, solicit, and resolve complaints is vital for long-term success.

> ### Customer Service Pledge
> United Airlines' employees and supervisors sign pledges that state: "No one will ever be punished for their efforts to solve a customer's problem."

Every company has, and will continue to have, complaints. If they don't, there is a *real* problem somewhere. Complaints are inevitable. The difference is in how those complaints are handled.

Complaint resolution *must* be swift, effective, caring, and reliable. The customer who complains loudly is the customer who is most apt to praise loudly. Complaining customers are not expendable. They are a treasure. They care enough for you and the company to give you the opportunity to do better.

Complaints are not resolved by companies. They are resolved by people. Individuals who understand and practice exceptional customer service will always be sought after and valued in the workplace. If you have the skills and the commitment to handle *all* complaints with an enthusiastic, confident and willing attitude, you have a marketable skill that is more precious than gold. Regardless of change, technology, downsizing, or economic conditions, you will be sought after, valued, and successful in any industry.

Turning complaints into compliments is money in the bank—for individuals and for their companies. Care about complaints and you'll turn concerns into compliments.

EXPLODE INTO ACTION

Forget mistakes. Forget failure. Forget everything except what you're going to do now, and do it.

—Will Durant

1 Collect the "easy" complaints. Ask all frontline people to contribute. Make it fun by having a competition for the "best" complaint.

2 Develop a plan to uncover the 96% of complaints that are never made by customers. Consider paying customers for complaints.

3 Do the same thing for internal customer complaints. Start by taking them privately since they will involve more internal politics.

4 Involve employees in developing a "manual" on how to handle complaints and things they can do to make it up to customers.

5 Train employees in helping unhappy customers, starting with saying "Thank you for complaining."

6 Clarify your lines of authority so any employee can deal quickly with most problems.

7 Develop a follow-up system to check in with customers who took the trouble to complain.

ONLINE CUSTOMER SERVICE: BUILDING A SENSE OF CONNECTION

Jeanette S. Cates

Jeanette S. Cates, PhD, aka The Technology Tamer™, specializes in helping people make friends with technology. As the founder and Head Tamer of TechTamers, a training and consulting firm based in Austin, Texas, Dr. Cates specializes in the planning, implementation, and assessment of technology in schools and the workplace. Some of her clients include Apple Computer, *Inc.* magazine, the San Diego Zoo, and the International Society for Technology in Education.

Noted for her fast-paced, computer-based presentations and her ability to explain complex concepts in an easy-to-understand manner, she is a frequent speaker at state and national conferences. She has developed more than 100 computer-based workshops, ranging from Presenting with Technology to Web-Page-in-a-Day™. She is a Certified Technical Trainer and holds credentials for numerous major software publishers. Dr. Cates is the author of many publications on multimedia and the Internet. Most recently she has written an online course on Web site design and is completing a book of the same title.

Dr. Cates is an active member of Women in Technology International, and serves as the Webmaster for the Heart of Texas chapter of the National Speakers Association.

Jeanette S. Cates, PhD, TechTamers, 10502 Hardrock, Austin, TX 78750; phone (512) 219-5653; fax(512) 219-5654; e-mail: cates@TechTamers.com; www.TechTamers.com.

ONLINE CUSTOMER SERVICE: BUILDING A SENSE OF CONNECTION

Jeanette S. Cates

> Computers have now made it possible to create an individual 'customer feedback loop,' integrating the . . . service delivery process into the research and promotion processes.
>
> —Don Peppers and Martha Rogers

As Don Peppers and Martha Rogers point out in their statement above, customer service can't be separated from your marketing and research. And they shouldn't be. The more you know about customers, the better service you can give them, and the more business they'll bring to you. Consider the following example.

Carolynn was looking for inexpensive airline tickets for herself and her children from San Francisco to Washington, DC. For weeks, she had been checking fares in newspapers and through various online services. It looked as if about $400 per ticket was the best deal going. One of the services through which she was monitoring airfares, TheTrip.com, provided a fare notification service. Carolynn registered to be notified (via e-mail) of low fares to the Washington area.

A couple of weeks later, she received an e-mail message from TheTrip saying that Southwest Airlines had a special $200 round-trip fare, but that since Southwest wasn't in the central airline reservation system, she would have to go to Southwest's Web site (address provided by TheTrip). TheTrip explained that although they could not provide the tickets in this case, they hoped she could use the information and would try TheTrip the next time she needed tickets.

E-MAIL FARE-SAVER ALERT!!!

Here's a great fare to your destination.

You won't be able to purchase these tickets through us (go to www.CompanyX.com)

Enjoy your trip!

Carolynn bought the tickets from Southwest, but made her rental car reservations through TheTrip. She was so impressed by TheTrip's putting her needs ahead of their own that TheTrip is now the only online travel service she uses and she has told the story to numerous friends and acquaintances.

This example shows how a company can use an automated online system to offer its customers timely and valuable information. It also shows how traditional concepts like loyalty marketing are just as potent in providing online customer service as in face-to-face interactions.

TRANSFORMED CUSTOMER SERVICE

According to a survey of department heads, 43.6% of customer service heads—more than any other department—said that Web technologies have increased the importance of their departments.

With the advent of the Internet, the landscape for customer service changed. Now there are unlimited opportunities for interaction with your customers.

Improvements from the Reps' Point of View

There are many stories of transformed customer service from online technologies. *Internet Week* gives an example of change from the service reps' point of view. Tony Ferrante is a rep at 1-800-Batteries. He says that closer customer interaction using e-mail has transformed his career for the better. "In the past, as a telephone customer rep, I felt my job was . . . kind of dull. I would come to work, sit down, and wait for the phone to ring. Now, I'm excited about my job, and I'm happy to have the chance to use my writing and analytical skills . . . I'm not limited to speaking to the customer for three minutes on the phone."

Regardless of where you are technologically, there is an online method that can enhance your customer service. If you're not offering it, your competitors will!

Benefits of Offering Online Service

First American National Bank sees these advantages in online service:

- reduced errors (because customers input their own information)
- lower costs for customer service (such as calls)
- increased sales
- decreased employee turnover (resulting from increased job satisfaction from more diverse work)

STRATEGY ONE: E-MAIL

The most obvious, and certainly the easiest electronic method of customer service is electronic mail or e-mail. Using e-mail you can send personal messages to individual customers. Or they can request information from you. Messages can be sent with the click of a button to a single individual or to hundreds, at a fraction of the cost of telephone calls or "snail mail."

An e-mail customer contact program, like any other program, takes preparation and training. Here are some suggestions for implementing an e-mail response system in your company.

Instant Responsiveness

CLICK HERE TO E-MAIL SERVICE REP

The uniqueness of e-mail is that it makes responding to a message easy. One click can get your customers' responses back to you—or yours to them. What could that instant interaction do for your service and research?

1. Decide who is going to receive the e-mail. Are you going to have a "triage" system where all e-mail comes to a single person, who then decides who will answer it? Or will you set up departments, with customers choosing the department to which the mail should be sent?

2. Set expectations for answering e-mail. Your customers expect speed. For example, your policy might be that all e-mail will be answered within two hours—or that an autoresponder will reply to e-mail immediately, with a personalized answer following within eight hours—or that an autoresponder will be the only response.

3. Create "boilerplate" responses to the more common questions. It will save your employees time and will ensure a standard response if they have answers that can be copied and pasted into their e-mail responses. Encourage them to personalize the standard responses in order to give customers that "special" feeling.

4. Train your employees on how to respond via e-mail. E-mail is a written correspondence. While less formal than a standard business letter, it is still considered an official reply from the company. Employees should be taught the same careful techniques as for any other correspondence. For monitoring purposes, you might have

What Is an Autoresponder?

An autoresponder automatically sends an e-mail response to incoming e-mail messages. For example, your customer service department might send the following message in response to each incoming e-mail:

Thank you for your e-mail. We appreciate your interest in Our Company. You will receive a personalized response within 8 hours.

Or if it is a holiday, your autoresponder might say:

We are celebrating Labor Day today and are out of the office. A customer service representative will return your e-mail tomorrow. Have a nice day!

An autoresponder can be quite sophisticated, recognizing the e-mail address or Web page that sent the message and sending a personalized message in response. For example, if an e-mail is from someone@xyz.com, your message might say:

We always appreciate interaction with employees of XYZ. You'll be hearing from us . . .

Or if the message is coming as a result of the Web page on ABC product, you might say:

We welcome your questions and comments on ABC . . ."

the supervisor receive a copy of all e-mail sent via a blind carbon copy. Or, rather than do it all of the time, have employees copy their supervisor during the probationary period and later only during specific periods (for example, the first and third Wednesdays of each month) so that the supervisor can keep up with the volume of e-mail.

4. Support your people. Provide typing instruction for your representatives if they are moving from telephone support to e-mail support. The volume of typing that you produce is directly related to your speed in keyboarding. They will be more receptive to the change if they are given the skills they need. At the same time, look at the equipment they are using. Are their computers fast enough? Are their keyboards placed at the correct angle? Are their monitors in the correct position? Are chairs ergonomically designed and adjusted for each employee?

5. Set standards for e-mail. For example:

a. All e-mail should have a subject.

b. Responses should repeat the question the customer asked.

c. Stick to a single topic for each e-mail response.

d. Watch your language. What can be expressed face-to-face can be more readily misinterpreted in writing. Read the message out loud before you send it to be sure there is no confusion over your meaning. If it is a particularly "sticky" situation, ask someone else to read it before you send it.

e. Use formatting to enhance the message. E-mail is most understandable when you write in short sentences, with space between paragraphs, and use indented lines.

f. Use a "signature file" that is added at the end of the message. This is a few lines of text that may include your name, position, telephone and fax numbers, company name and slogan, and Web site address. Be sure you decide ahead of time what you want to put in this file and standardize it for all employees. You may not want them to use their names and phone numbers because of the impact additional calls would have.

6. Be sure to capture information on customers who use e-mail. You should be able to tie their e-mail addresses to any other registration or marketing lists that you have. Ideally, you'll want to link their e-mail questions and comments to their record. That way you can see everything they purchased from you, past problems, comments they made, or testimonials they offered. You can use the data you glean from e-mail messages to choose focus groups, groups to whom you'll

More on Autoresponders: A Caution and Other Options

When using an autoresponder, be sure you get back to the customer when you say you will. An autoresponder message may be interpreted as the same thing as being put "on hold" with your telephone system. Imagine being put on hold for 24 hours! It can seem like an eternity when you need an answer.

Consider extending the information provided in an autoresponder. For example, your first "thank you for your e-mail" message might include FAQs (a list of answers to Frequently Asked Questions). Or it may contain hyperlinks (blue, underlined text that when clicked, brings up a Web page) to the information at your Web site.

Remember, it does not cost any more in electronic space to send a long message than to send a short one. Providing a longer response may enable your customers to answer their own questions. Customers are happy because their problems get solved quicker—and your customer service reps have more time to deal with more complicated problems.

Make It Personal

My name's Dan. I'll be your customer service rep.

If you provide customer service on the telephone, customers like to know that they can call "their" representative and get a personal response. The same is true online. Consider assigning a personal customer service representative to each customer. A customer can send e-mail directly to this representative. It cuts down on each employee having to deal with the total breadth of the customer base and lets them get to know customers better.

One of the drawbacks to this approach is employee turnover. Handle this by assigning representative names on a permanent basis, regardless of the actual employee who responds. For example, dan@yourcorp.com may be Betty for two months, then Jorge for the next three. The customers don't have to be inconvenienced just because you had a change in personnel.

market a new product, or groups to whom you'll send upgrade or recall information. No e-mail data should escape your customer database.

Outbound E-mail

One of the major focuses of online communication with your customers should be to build relationships with them so that they feel part of your "community." By increasing the frequency of contact and the value of information sent to them, you can make them feel a part of your world. Just make sure that most of your contacts are not self-serving so that customers see the benefits to them.

One of the most common means of staying in touch with customers is an electronic newsletter (ezine) sent on a regular basis. Some companies have a weekly e-mail newsletter, but many prefer monthly distribution.

If you choose weekly distribution, keep it short. Most people do not have time or a desire to read a long e-mail letter from you every week. Monthly newsletters are popular as a means of updating customers. Include information of value to them (for example, tips and tricks, new products, special sales, creative uses of the product), not just commercials.

Three excellent examples take different approaches to the e-mail newsletter.

The *Guerrilla Marketing On-line Weekly* (www.gmarketing.com) presents a one- or two-sentence summary of each article, then gives you the link to the entire article at their Web site. Since it's weekly, it would be too much to print every article in the body of the newsletter. Besides, they want you to come to their Web site!

Mike McCann's Building Your Business newsletter (www.comperfect.com) is published monthly on his Web site. He then sends a personalized e-mail to each subscriber, telling them it has been published and giving the table of contents for the current issue. The Web address is included.

Terri Lonier of *Working Solo* (www.workingsolo.com) publishes a monthly newsletter that has the articles in the body of the e-mail. She adopts a personal perspective so that you feel as if she is talking to you. When she mentions a Web site, she includes the address so that you can hyperlink to it. It is a monthly. Because of the personalized feel and the high quality information she includes, the length of the newsletter is not intrusive.

Daily Contact

Another approach to sending e-mail to customers is in the form of daily tips. Daily tips are small, digestible ideas. Because they contain only a single thought, they are a very effective follow-up to new learning. I set up daily tips for many of the workshops I present. These remind participants of what they learned, reinforce an idea they heard, review a technique they heard but didn't internalize, or introduce them to new concepts.

Ask, Ask, Ask!

Ask your customers what they want. Would they prefer the answers to their questions via e-mail, fax, or standard mail?

Most people prefer to hear from you in the same way in which they sent the question. But it never hurts to ask. Would they rather register their product online or use the mail-back card? Send short surveys via their preferred method of communication, asking them about products, services, and other issues.

Again, *Guerrilla Marketing* shows a good example of the daily "tips." For less than $10 per year, you can receive three daily guerrilla tips—about sales, marketing, and online marketing. Another excellent daily tip sheet comes from Stacy Brice of Virtual Assistant University (www. assistu.com). She provides a Daily Assistant update with a quote, a word of the day, and a technique that enhances your in-office efficiency. She also provides an option for a weekly digest of the daily information, if daily is too frequent for you.

Set the Expectation

Include a space for your customer's e-mail address on your product registration card. When you receive a customer's card, send back a welcome message via e-mail. Develop a plan to e-mail information to your customers on a regular basis. Your customers will soon expect to hear from you via e-mail.

Finally, e-mail should be sent to all of your customers when you upgrade the product they own, announce a new service, have a significant earnings increase, or have other noteworthy news. Remember that your overall strategy should be one of inclusion—in your "family" or community—at the same time that you are providing information.

A word of caution on outbound e-mail: Always make it easy for the customer to turn it "off." At the bottom of each message include the instructions on how to discontinue the subscription.

STRATEGY TWO: YOUR WEB SITE

If you are using e-mail, you probably already have a Web site or are well on your way. Most commercial Web sites are designed as marketing tools. They highlight the services and products provided by the company. They are designed to attract new customers, but are not necessarily set up to support existing customers.

Differentiate Between Customers and Prospects

While a single Web site may be usable for both prospects and customers, you need to look at it from a customer's perspective when you are discussing customer service. Make sure your site, or a section of it, is designed for your existing customers. They are more valuable to you than prospects.

What are some of the differences?

How do you best meet the needs of your customers? You may incorporate their needs into your existing Web site or you may set up a separate Web site for them. When you create an external Web site dedicated to your customers, it is referred to as an "extranet," as opposed to an "intranet" (for internal use) and the "Internet" (for the general public).

"Well, Max, we're ready to go. We got our fish, we got our ice, and our Web site is online."

While you may decide not to establish a separate extranet at this time, you may want to password-protect part of your current Web site so that only existing customers can use the resources behind the password. This creates a feeling of community among those who have the password and often generates a compulsion to "join the community" for those who are considering purchasing. This can be a strong selling point—"an exclusive Web site dedicated to our customers."

The FAQs

The first document to post on your Web site for both customers and prospects is a Frequently Asked Questions (FAQ) document. The FAQ is a list of questions and answers. The questions are

Dell Customizes Web Pages for Each Customer

People wonder why Dell computers is able to sell a billion dollars of computers online. One big reason is that they create a customized Web site for each of their big customers.

For instance, Dell will have Fortune 500 Company X's purchasing forms on the Dell Web site. Then when Company X needs to order a computer, it can order from Dell's Web site as quickly and easily as ordering from its own stockroom!

usually listed in some type of table of contents, either at the top of the page or on a prior page. You will probably establish several FAQs—some for those considering the purchase of a product; others for those who already own the product and want to know about the how-to's. If yours is a complex product, you will have many pages of FAQs.

FAQs are easily created using the database of questions that your current customer service representatives answer on a daily basis. Export these questions to a new document and format it for the Web and you have your first FAQ. To capture more questions and answers, meet regularly with your frontline operators who receive the questions, or set up a process to add new questions to the FAQ as they are added to the database.

FAQs may be included or referenced in an automatic response to an e-mail question. Customers can often find their answers in the FAQs, but don't think to check them before sending a message. Likewise, the FAQ may provide the basis for the standard answers that are sent via e-mail.

Customize

Consider including personalized information for your customers. Generally you will do this by having them complete an online form that lets them identify their interests, product purchases, and other information that can give you information about the type of information they want. Then, each time they sign in you are able to greet them personally and provide information customized for them.

The main benefit to this customized approach is that they do not have to look through information that does not interest them in trying to locate the information that does. It saves them time and effort. From your perspective, it provides more information than you would have gotten from a registration card and lets you customize your future marketing efforts.

However, there are drawbacks to customization. Customers have to take the time to register. Also, you either have to use a "cookie" technology (see box on the next page) or customers must sign in each time they enter the site. This may take more time and effort than customers are willing to put in, unless you can provide them unique services and information they can't find elsewhere. For example, American Express (www.americanexpress. com) lets you check your card charges online.

STRATEGY THREE: WHAT TO PUT ON YOUR SITE

Customer Testimonials

Satisfied customers love to tell their stories. Consider creating a submission area where they

---

Design Your Web Site for Your Customers

Some Web sites look like they are designed for the glory of the organization, not for the ease of use of the customer. Keep the following considerations in mind when designing your Web site.

1. How new are their computers? If they are older than 2 years, they probably need a 640 × 480 pixel display.

2. How fast are their modems? Most home-based users have 28.8 modems, with some of them just starting to upgrade to 56K. On the other hand, most corporate customers are connecting through a direct line at high speeds. Be sure you test your pages at the speeds your customers use. If you are designing on a high-speed line and your customers are downloading information on a 28.8 modem, you are not meeting their needs.

3. Do they want to print copies of your information? If so, design the pages so that they fit on a standard page of paper. Too often pages are designed for the wider 1024 × 768 pixel size and will not fit on the paper without turning it to landscape (sideways). This is irritating to your customers. Consider formatting your FAQ pages on plain backgrounds at the narrower page size so that they are fast to print.

If in doubt, ASK your customers. They will be glad to tell you what works for them and what doesn't.

Want Some Cookies?

You may have seen a warning that lets you know a cookie was being loaded onto your computer. Online "cookies" are small files that are placed on your computer by a Web site. They contain information about your preferences at that particular site. Many cookies are temporary and exist only as long as you are connected to a site; others disappear when you log off the Internet. Permanent cookies are stored in your computer and let a Web site know who you are when you arrive at that site again.

Many people think they can catch a virus from cookies or that someone can connect and steal information from your hard drive using your cookie. This is not the case. For a full discussion of cookies, check Cookie Central at http://www.cookiecentral.com.

can tell how they are using your product. Then use what they've written to highlight your customers as your success stories. Prospects will be impressed and current customers may get new ideas or decide to submit their successes. Be sure to link success stories to the Web sites of your customers. This enhances that sense of connectedness in your community.

Search Engines

One of the key enhancements you can provide to a customer Web site is a search engine. Rather than having to click through six or seven layers of linked documents, customers can put in the keywords they are looking for and go directly to what they want. This feature says that you value their time and want to be as responsive online as possible.

Tracking

Use the built-in tracking from the Web to determine areas where customers need more support. By measuring the number of "hits" a particular area receives, you can determine if everyone is looking at the same pages. Likewise, you can see if a large number of users leave the site after a particular page, indicating they either found what they were looking for or gave up.

Secure Ordering

Expand the sales of parts and upgrades while serving your customers by providing an online ordering system. Make it easy for customers to find the product they have and any related information about it—updates, upgrades, frequently asked questions, and tips for use. By providing online ordering, you not only save on the number of representatives you need to provide, but you are also able to provide the service 24-hours a day, without an increased cost. Customers can order their parts and upgrades regardless of their

Keep Your Web Site Fresh

It is important to keep all Web sites current, but especially important when your Web site is aimed at customers who will make repeat visits to your site. It is important for customers to find something new each time they come. Plan to update information daily—weekly at the least. Enter new information at the top of each section, so customers will see the new information first.

time zone. Service online is cheaper for you and more convenient for your customers.

STRATEGY FOUR: ONLINE LEARNING

If you service a complex product or service, you may want to provide opportunities for continued learning or applications. Adobe® (www.adobe.com) does a good job of this with their online tips and techniques. In these tip sheets, they show how to use a single product in a specific way. For example, they provide an activity sheet on how to design a black-and-white yellow pages ad using their PhotoDeluxe® product. You are walked through the process of using the product and some of its features. Not only do they show a technique to their existing customers, but they also provide the link to purchase the product for prospects.

A more advanced type of learning is available from other companies. The Apple Learning Interchange (www.apple.com/education/ali) serves the education community. In a recent online survey, ALI members said they were interested in expanding their skills by taking online courses and identified the top eight topics they wanted to study. In response, ALI provides six-week courses that include lessons, projects, and interaction among the enrolled students. Not only do the online offerings generate revenue, but more importantly they provide a service in response to customers' requests.

Use Multimedia

One of the biggest enhancements to online learning is the use of multimedia. You can add an audio track to static pictures so that users can listen to the instructions, instead of having to read them. Better yet, you can offer a video of the procedure, so that they can watch before they use it themselves.

> Information is not the key, knowledge is. What really moves the marketplace is knowledge or the lack of it. . . . Knowledge that educates helps move a product to the user. Lack of knowledge prevents action and, in fact, reduces sales.
> —Ray Jutkins, *Power Direct Marketing*

As with all technology, however, use these advanced techniques cautiously. They often involve special software and computer capabilities that not all of your customers have. If you offer them, make them optional with the plain text-and-pictures instructions there as well. You'll serve a much broader base of clients that way and they will appreciate the fact that you have not left them behind in the quest for new technologies.

STRATEGY FIVE: INTERACTIVE SERVICE

The more involvement you can offer your customers, the more likely they are to become a part of your community. E-mail is a one-way technology, where only one person can talk at a time. Web sites are also one-way, with the customer interacting with relatively static pages. Even online learning is often one-way, with information presented to the customer, and responses sent to the company. To move to more dynamic interaction, you will need to add another level of technology to your online presence. There are two major categories of interactive sites: asynchronous (delayed) and synchronous (live).

Listservs

The most common type of asynchronous communication is actually a relative of e-mail. It is the "listserv." On a listserv, every subscriber can contribute to the conversation. They do so by sending e-mail to a central address. The central address, in turn, echoes that out to all members of the listserv.

The advantage to a listserv from a customer service perspective is that all members can participate. Often members will answer each other's questions, saving the time of your representatives. You should normally "moderate" the discussion. This means you check each contribution to make sure it is relevant, rather than advertising or personal attacks.

The biggest drawback is that a listserv is still delayed communication. In addition, some customers may not subscribe and of those who do, they may find their e-mail boxes filled with unrelated information. One way around this disadvantage is to archive the listserv on your Web site. That way, customers who don't want to receive the e-mail can still read the discussions at their leisure. Of course, this is no different than the FAQs and other materials you have provided on your Web site—and may not present nearly as positive a spin as your marketing materials. If you do archive your discussion groups, I strongly recommend you use the search engine on your site so that it's easier to find information, rather than wading through all of the messages.

A relative of a listserv is the message board. Again, this gives customers a place to discuss issues related to your products and to exchange

---

Where to Find Online Discussions and Newsletters

Other directories of online discussion lists and newsletters:

www.site-city.com

http://ezinesearch.com

www.meer.net/~john/e-zine-list

www.gizmonet.com/pubform.htm

www.listz.com

www.onelist.com

www.listserv.com

www.majordomo.com

tips and techniques. A message board takes more initiative on the part of customers because they must log onto the message board and read and type there. So while a listserv delivers the discussion to their e-mail box, a message board is like a bulletin board—you have to go down the hall to read it.

In both the case of a listserv and a message board, you need to assign an employee to monitor and contribute to the discussions. This is critical to monitoring customer comments and to being sure the correct information is presented to the group. Likewise, if there are newsgroups on the Internet that involve your industry or your product, you will want to be sure someone from your company checks those regularly. To search the list of newsgroups, check with www.dejanews.com.

> If you have an unhappy customer on the Internet, he doesn't tell his six friends, he tells his 6,000 friends.
> —Jeff Bezos, president, Amazon.com

Chat Rooms

The synchronousinteractive technologies available to you online include chat rooms. These chats let users type messages into a window. Everyone else connected to that chat room can read that message live. Chat rooms have been credited with the widespread success of America Online. They have also gained a seedy reputation in some circles, when they are allowed to go unmonitored and without guidelines. So the first thing you will need to consider if you provide a chat room for live discussions is a monitoring system.

Generally, you can assign a customer care representative to monitor the chat room when it is open. Note, too, that you can close a chat room when you do not want it used. You may want to announce specific topics that will be discussed at a particular time.

Web Center

One of the most effective applications of the chat room concept is WebCenter® by Acuity (www.acuity.com). As a customer goes to a customer service site using WebCenter, they are welcomed and invited to submit a question. The WebCenter software interprets their question and searches in the FAQs and product knowledge base using artificial intelligence. The software offers several potential answers that the customer is then free to explore further.

If none of the answers is satisfactory, the customer passes into a live cue. Here a company representative will chat with the customer on a live basis, sometimes offering to respond by phone or e-mail to answer a question that takes additional research.

In contrast to all other methods of online response which are delayed, WebCenter offers the opportunity to have a question answered immediately through the software or by a representative using live chat. This immediacy, combined with the ability to track information requests, percentage of satisfactory responses from the knowledge base, and the number of requests that must be resolved by an agent, provide the type of system that many believe will be the future of online customer service.

> ## Hold Auditorium Events
>
> If you want to offer an online chat with a "big name" personality in your industry, you may use a variation of a chat room called an auditorium. In the auditorium, everyone can hear the person on the stage, but the audience cannot chat among themselves. They can ask questions, however. The questions are passed on to the speaker who answers them for the audience as a whole.

Conferencing

Another type of chat software that ties to the learning formats discussed in the prior section is conferencing software. This software allows two or more locations to communicate via video or audio. It may or may not include a "white board" for showing or exchanging ideas.

The benefit of conferencing software, of course,

is that it draws the parties closer together by providing a more realistic interface than typing words back and forth. However, the major drawback is that it requires both parties to have the same type of software. While this may not be practical for the general public, you should certainly consider using it for specialized, high-end products, or for special groups of customers. For those customers, you can ship or install the necessary software for all parties so that it is ready to use when necessary.

Web-Based Customer Service Pays

- Forrester Research estimates that Web-based support will save the typical business up to 43% in labor costs by the year 2000
- Analysts estimate that a straightforward request, handled on the phone costs a company between $25 and $30. By comparison, resolving the same problem through Web-based self-service applications costs between $2 and $3 (from www.silknet.com).
- Customers tend to ask the same questions over and over again. Analysts estimate that repetition is as high as the 50–70% range (from www.silknet.com).

SUMMARY

Online technology is here to stay. Even though it is advancing very fast, the examples I've discussed will help you get started or improve your service online. By now, everyone should be using e-mail. But you may not have procedures for your customer interactions. Similarly, you may have a Web site, but not reviewed it with customer service in mind.

Regardless of where you are in your quest to provide better customer service through the use of online technologies, remember several guidelines:
- Ask your customers, then listen to their responses.
- Develop your plan carefully.
- Implement slowly.
- Plan to provide ongoing training and feedback for your employees.
- Advertise your online capabilities through print and other media.

BURST INTO ACTION

We cannot do everything at once,
but we can do something at once.
—Calvin Coolidge

1 Create a policy on how to use e-mail to help your customers.

2 Set high standards for speed of response to e-mail correspondence. Look into using autoresponders for immediate responses.

3 Analyze your Web site from your customers' perspective. Prepare a FAQ page if you don't already have one.

4 Create standard letters (boilerplate) from your best answers to questions for all reps to use.

5 Create a way to communicate on a regular basis with customers who wish it, such as an online newsletter or discussion group.

6 Personalize messages whenever possible. (There are products that allow even e-mail newsletters to be personally addressed.)

7 Look into the benefits of customizing an extranet for all customers, or individually for major customers.

8 Consider providing online courses or other online learning opportunities for customers.

9 Set up a schedule to regularly update your Web site.

CROSS-CULTURAL CUSTOMER SERVICE FOR THE 21st CENTURY
Are You Prepared?

Patricia Zakian Tith

Patricia Zakian Tith,
MS Sociolinguistics, MS Education, is a speaker, seminar leader, and management consultant. As a sociolinguist, she understands the interactions of diversity, culture, and language and how they play out in today's multicultural workplaces.

She has extensive experience working with organizations that need to have constructive communications across cultures in all aspects of their businesses as well as be competitive in the global marketplace. Her clients have included corporations (AT&T, Dupont), associations (American Society of Association Executives, Food Marketing Institute), government agencies (U.S. Foreign Service Institute, Chinese Academy of Sciences), international organizations (World Bank, World Health Organization), and universities (George Washington University). She is president of Global Workplace Dynamics.

She has traveled extensively throughout the world—including living and working in France and China. To add to her knowledge, she has interviewed managers and employees in more than 60 joint ventures, foreign subsidiaries, and large- to medium-sized firms in Belarus, China, Estonia, France, Hungary, Laos, Latvia, Russia, and the United States.

Patricia Zakian Tith, Global Workplace Dynamics, 2400 Virginia Avenue NW, Suite C312, Washington, DC 20037; phone (202) 293-7748; fax (202) 466-3376; www.globalworkplace.com.

CROSS-CULTURAL CUSTOMER SERVICE FOR THE 21st CENTURY
Are You Prepared?

Patricia Zakian Tith

> The Platinum Rule™ goes beyond the golden rule. Don't treat people the way *you* want to be treated, treat them the way *they* want to be treated.
>
> —Tony Alessandra, *The Platinum Rule*

C ulture is a key element in understanding what is behind the variety of customer responses and reactions. Do you know enough about that person on the other end of the customer service conversation? Who is behind that handshake? Who is behind that smile? Who is behind that complaint?

If you can't come up with confident answers to those questions, please read on. You need to upgrade your approach to customer service as we move into the 21st century.

THE NEW REALITY—
A MULTICULTURAL MARKETPLACE

Joe Cossman, promoter of the ant farm and many other items, tells this story about cultural differences. He was on a foreign cruise ship and had given a gift to his steward. Later, he admired a clay dog that his steward had bought in India. The steward gave it to him. Cossman then gave the steward another gift, who gave him another gift. Eventually, the steward said, "Please, Mr. Cossman, no more gifts." As the customer, Cossman had wanted to be generous to the steward. But, the steward was operating under norms that required reciprocity, and he could no longer afford the gift-giving!

Culture determines how we behave and interact with others. Although there are many definitions and uses for the word "culture," the essence of all of them comes down to "the way we do things around here." It is the shared way of life of a group of people. It is the "software" of our minds—our internal programming.

Cultural Software

To function in a society, we need software—a language of verbal and nonverbal cues, and a shared history—that enables us to interact in a social context. This software allows us to communicate with other individuals who are using the same rules.

Remember just a few years back, when personal computers were in their infancy. Back then, if you used Microsoft Word and a colleague used Wordperfect, you couldn't read each others' files (unless you stripped away all formatting). As software programming progressed, filters were added to software to allow one program to read files created by another, and keep the formatting (cues

> From the moment of his birth, the customs into which [an individual] is born shape his experience and behavior. By the time he can talk, he is the little creature of his culture.
> —Ruth Fulton Benedict, *Patterns of Culture*

like boldface, italics, special characters) intact.

Imagine that someone sends you the message "Keep **ME** informed of the changes," but you receive the message without formatting ("Keep me informed of the changes"). You might reasonably assume that it would be okay to pass notification of the changes along to anyone in the sender's office, when, in fact, the sender meant the formatting to convey that notification be directly to her.

It is the same with our internal software. If we are using Anglo Saxon software, we will likely have trouble communicating with people who use Chinese software. It is like reading a word processing file with all the formatting stripped away. Without the cues that the formatting provides, misinterpretations are more likely to happen. We need to upgrade our software to recognize that differences exist. Then we need to add filters that allow us to recognize and interpret messages sent from different software (cultures) than ours.

> Facts mean nothing unless they are rightly understood, rightly related and rightly interpreted.
> —R.L. Long

Cultural—and Everyday—Changes

Today's reality in the marketplace reflects the changing face of the customer, the way products are made, and the intense competition for market share. Concepts like globalization, multicultural marketing, and a borderless world are commonly used to describe the impact of diversity in the types of customers and their tastes, habits, and preferences.

What does this mean for customer service? It means that the marketplace has changed and will continue to change.

Consequently, customer service is not what it used to be. Today's customers, both domestically and internationally, are not homogenous and predictable groups as in the past. The same old customer service strategies targeted towards a mass marketplace will no longer be as effective as they once were. These changes leave both mass marketing and mass customer service in the dust! An additional level of sophistication will be required to remain competitive and grow market share.

> ## Multicultural Realty
>
> The Rancho Los Cerritos Board of Realtors in California sponsored a seminar on how different ethnic groups choose houses. To give the best service, real estate agents need to know about cultural differences. For instance, Filipinos don't want stairways with a number of steps divisible by three. Some Chinese don't like the front and back doors of a house to face each other. Indians often prefer a front door that faces east. In any business, learning about different cultures can give you a service edge.

Customer-Service Changes

Some of the factors at work driving this new customer service environment are:

- social roles are no longer clear cut
- more women are in the workplace
- multiculturalism is impacting tastes and cultural habits
- customers are more demanding and particular
- customers are more educated
- customers place a premium on time
- customers have technology to explore options to maximize satisfaction
- technology has brought more international customers
- competition is global

Your marketplace is no longer limited to one subculture. Given this new marketplace reality, how can you satisfy the different cultural needs and habits of your customers in order to keep their loyalty? Said another way, how can you "hear" the voices of this diversity in your customer base to ensure a long-term relationship? You can do this by being more knowledgeable in your approach to customer service.

HOW TO BENEFIT FROM CULTURAL DIFFERENCES

What do you need to do to upgrade your customer service? How can you lock in your market share, your competitive advantage, and your customers' loyalty? How can you make connections with these diverse and multicultural customers? What follows are some guidelines to help you gain customer service enlightment.

Understand the Role of Culture in the Marketplace

Understanding the role of culture may sound obvious, but remember that it has been proven time and time again that the most obvious human behavior can be the most important as well as the most difficult to "see" and *understand*.

Every individual has unique qualities. Subcultures can differ. Organizations have their unique ways as well. Overhanging both of these is the national culture. Even though some people like to think they are totally unique unto themselves, they are operating within the cultural norms of their national culture. Americans have their norms of behaving, as do the Germans, Chinese, Nigerians, Hispanics, and so forth.

The cultural norms governing behavior are *less* obvious within the context of a national culture, as, for example, *among* Americans in the U.S. They only become an issue when there is a clash with another culture (such as the Japanese). At such times, the individuals involved may not realize what is happening. They will most likely attribute the clash to a defect in the other individual.

America has many faces. Some I understand and some I don't. Those I don't understand I never judge or express an opinion about.

—Vaclev Havel, President, Czech Republic Press conference, September 1998

Characteristics of Culture

Imagine an iceberg. The tip is visible (like the tangible parts of culture). The rest of the iceberg is below the water level and is basically a mystery like the invisible parts of culture. It is very difficult to know size and movements. This is the same for human behavior. The invisible aspects of culture are hidden within the individual. Not to recognize this fact could lead to major disasters in customer service. What you see, may not be what you think you see.

The visible parts of culture are such things as food, dress, architecture, the arts, music, and literature. All of these are the tangible aspects of culture, there for us to see and touch. We don't see the intangible aspects—values, beliefs, assumptions, attitudes, customs—that drive all our behavior. The only way to deal with these behavioral "drivers" for better customer service is to (a) look for differences and ask customers about them, (b) factor them into any interaction with a customer when appropriate.

Here are some facts about cultures and subcultures that are important:

1. Culture is learned and is not innate. Culture and the resulting socialization are acquired through contact and association with others who have a shared view of how people should behave. Our parents, along with the schools and other societal institutions, transmit not only national culture but also the cultures of subgroups. For example, parents of Armenian heritage in the U.S. will pass on aspects of both Armenian and American cultural norms to their children as they grow up.

2. Culture determines what we see and feel. Perception is culturally determined. It is learned behavior. Perception affects what we see and don't see. Even people from the same cultural background see things differently because percep-

> We don't see things as they are, we see them as we are.
> —Anais Nin

> Our old views constrain us. They deprive us of engaging fully with this universe of potentialities.
> —Margaret Wheatley

tion is dependent not only on cultural background but also on such factors as profession, age, social position, education, predispositions to this or that, and so on. It depends on where you are coming from.

What you know and are familiar with is what you will "see." An expert sailor will look at a harbor full of sailboats and be able to distinguish one class of sailboats from another. A neophyte will just see the generic sailboats. Wine is just wine to a nonconnoisseur; but to an wine afficianado, there are many elements to determine what makes a good wine.

In the area of customer service, if you have to deal with customers from a variety of national or ethnic backgrounds, you will not easily be able to detect what is really being communicated because of a lack of knowledge about cultural norms. Customer service staff will only be able to see, hear, and perceive messages that are familiar to them.

3. Culture influences *all* behavior. It is impossible to stand back and objectively view your own culture because its influence is pervasive and subtle. Likewise, it is very difficult to be an objective and impartial viewer of another culture.

Culture is like the lenses in a pair of glasses. What you see is dependent on what lenses you are looking through (your particular prescription). You can't see well through someone else's glasses because the prescription is different. When an American interacts and communicates with a Chinese customer, the American views the interactions through American cultural lenses

---

Cultural Differences in Music Appreciation

A typical American multimedia firm might put together the most polished slide show, videotape, or motion picture money can buy, with lots of action and music. But your Arabic audience won't like it. Why not? Maybe your presentation is in English rather than in Arabic. Or perhaps the music selected is inappropriate (music is a form of entertainment in the Arab culture and is unacceptable in many business presentations).

and the Chinese customer views the same interaction through Chinese cultural lenses—the Chinese cultural prescription. Neither one can wear the other's glasses and expect to see properly.

4. There is no such thing as "truth" from a cultural perspective. While some cultures are more effective in some situations, to feel that your way is the only way is to push yourself up against a wall. Common sense is not "common" to everyone. What is logical is culturally determined. The trick is to determine what the other peson's logic or rationale is. Is it Japanese, Italian, or American logic? If you don't know, you need to do a quick study and find out if you want to provide more effective customer service.

CULTURAL DRIVERS

Cultural drivers guide our "cultural" behavior. Without them there would be no code or structure shared by a group of people and no way to interact with others in your group so that everyone will understand. Cultural drivers include verbal and nonverbal communication, communication style, attitudes toward time, the role of the individual in society, and levels of formality.

1. Verbal language. Behind every word we use is a concept that is culturally defined. The meaning of very familiar words can have enough differences across groups to cause communication barriers. In politics, democracy has different meanings across cultures. In the workplace, words like service,

How We React to the Unfamiliar

Typical reactions to things unfamiliar are:

- assuming a position of superiority—our way is the best way
- becoming ethnocentric—I don't like you and your way, so end of story
- assuming there is a universal way (my way)—for all humans
- fear of strangeness, leading to flight or hostility

These reactions become barriers to effective communications with your customers. They close down your ability to really hear what the customer is saying. You are being blinded by your cultural software when you have such reactions. It is interfering with your ability to be reasonably impartial and objective.

conflict, leadership, and deadline do not have uniform meanings to all cultures. Words vary in their meanings not only among subgroups of Americans, but also among other national cultures. Therefore, one cannot assume that you and your customer are operating on the same conceptual basis when you are providing service.

The expectations of your customer may not be met by the words you are using in the delivery of service. This results in confusion, delay, irritation, frustration, and even the ultimate loss of the customer.

The enlightened customer service specialist must be careful *not* to assume anything. In working with diverse populations, one must get used to routinely clarifying and double checking meanings to make sure real understanding is taking place. By doing this regularly, you will be able to offer the best possible customer service because you will really be communicating.

Communications to the Global Market

Remember these guidelines when customers have limited knowledge of English:

• Use short, simple sentences.
• Avoid idioms and slang.
• Restate important or complex messages several ways.

—Roger E. Axtell,
Do's and Taboos of International Trade

2. Nonverbal language. Nonverbal language reveals a lot of information. It can be eye contact, facial expressions, gestures, body movements, or posture. For the most part, nonverbal language is delivered unconsciously. Sometimes, the emotional content of a message is delivered more strongly nonverbally than verbally. This is why it is critical to have some basic understanding of what key nonverbal behaviors mean in the different cultures of your customers so you can be effective in delivering service.

A smile is not always a signal of happiness or friendliness as most Americans would interpret it. In Asian cultures, a smile tends to convey nervousness and embarrassment. If you are aware of this, you can try to figure out what is going on by questioning and clarifying what has just taken place to cause this reaction.

The Japanese are well known for their lengthy pauses before responding. This can disrupt the flow of ideas and conversation for an American who is culturally conditioned to shorter pauses. Silence for Americans is very offputting. For the Japanese, it is not. They use silence along with head nodding in the communication process. Silence in the Japanese context is more often than not reflecting a favorable impression and is showing that deep thought is being given to the subject being discussed.

3. Communication style. Differences in communication styles can be the root of many problems in customer service.

Total communication is more than just verbal and nonverbal aspects. Cultures can generally be put into two groups. High-context cultures send information not only via words but also via status, nonverbal language, and their relationships with people. Asia, Latin American, Africa, and the Middle East are high context regions. For these groups, it is not advisable to be explicit and direct in what you say.

In customer service, this results in:

- indirect communication—implicitly stated
- business relationships built on trust and past interactions
- importance of status and the group

 Cultural Differences

Most French workers would believe they were imposing if they offered to socialize with an American co-worker. Being late for a business meeting in Germany or Sweden is a deadly insult to the person you're meeting—you're unlikely to have any future business dealings. French business meetings are considered a place to simply randomly throw around ideas—real decision making is done privately. When the French lose their tempers, they simply consider it a way of communicating and it holds low significance. French and Japanese businesses find it hard to believe that win-win contracts are possible, so they look for problems.

—*International Herald Triibune*

- subtle handling of conflict and disagreement
- importance of nonverbal communication

Low-context cultures depend on words for getting information. Information is more clearly and specifically spelled out. Relationships start and end more quickly. Conflicts are depersonalized. North America, Australia, and Northern Europe are low-context regions. Southern Europe is in the middle.

In customer service, this results in:

- direct communication clearly and explicitly stated
- business relationships less dependent on trust and more focused on the task at hand
- identity more rooted in self than in a group
- information directly exchanged

> Mad dogs and Englishmen go
> out in the mid-day sun;
> The Japanese don't care to,
> the Chinese wouldn't dare to;
> Hindus and Argentines sleep
> firmly from twelve to one,
> But Englishmen detest a
> Siesta . . .
>
> –Noel Coward

4. Attitude towards time. The way people perceive and use time is *not* universal. Edward Hall, the anthropologist, found that cultures are either monochronic or polychronic in the way they regard time.

In monochronic cultures like the U.S., Canada, and most of northern Europe:

- time is linear—one thing at a time
- commitment to schedules, promptness, and deadlines
- action orientation
- more concentrated on the future
- less flexible with time—they separate work from play
- time is a commodity

In the U.S., an 11:00 appointment means arriving five minutes before and starting business at 11:00 or a few minutes later.

In polychronic cultures like the Middle East, Africa, Latin America, Southern Europe, and, to some extent, Asia, people tend to believe that:

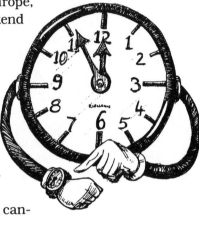

- time is circular, not limited
- there is always time to concentrate on relationships which are central and highly valued
- schedules and deadlines can always be adjusted.
- several things can be accomplished at the same time
- the future is not certain and cannot be planned
- time is a continuum

Plans are frequently changed since maintaining relationships always takes priority over a strict schedule. Appointments tend to start late because people tend to arrive late. It is common for meetings to go on longer than planned because of the importance of relationships.

Hispanics are more comfortable discussing many things at the same time, while Americans like to discuss one thing at a time in an orderly and linear way. In Latin America, the attitude is less rigid. Delays of 30 minutes or more are neither alarming nor surprising. This cultural difference in viewing time is recognized and is called "la hora española" (the Latin hour) versus la hora inglesa (the English hour).

5. The role of the individual in society. In the cultures of Australia, North America, and Europe, the individual and individualism are highly valued. "I" predominates over "we" in conversations. The expression "The squeaky wheel gets the grease" shows the importance of the individual. People are expected to speak up and be heard. Customers are independent and are expected to take care of themselves. Central to social control are guilt and the fear of loss of self-respect. Laws and rights are the same for everyone. Political power rests with individuals. Treat customers as individuals and expect them to speak up for themselves.

In the cultures of Africa, Latin America, the Middle East, and Asia, the group is much more valued than the individual. "We" predominates over "I" in conversations. The expression "The nail that sticks up is hammered down" shows the importance of the collective group. Harmony rather than speaking one's mind is a key value. Customers often will not tell you when there is a problem.

Individual interests are subordinate to the group's interests. The individual is protected by the group in exchange for obedience and loyalty. Identity comes from the social group to which the individual belongs. Social control comes from the fear of a loss of face and shame. Show respect for the group to which the individual belongs.

American Cultural Drivers

The cultural drivers of mainstream Americans are:
- use of direct and open communication
- belief in the individual
- informality
- equalitarian in dealing with people
- change is positive
- time is money
- relationships not overly important
- use of schedules and deadlines
- friendly

6. Level of formality.

Informal cultures place less value on protocol and social customs than do formal cultures. People from informal cultures feel more comfortable without ceremony and, therefore, value a casual and friendly atmosphere. The U.S. and Australia are considered by many to be the most informal cultures in the world. The American style of customer service is "close" and friendly. Efficiency is important because people are usually paid for results.

Canada and New Zealand are informal, but less so than the U.S. or Australia.

Formal cultures put a strong emphasis on protocol and social customs. There exists a strong sense of history, tradition, and culture. They feel that decorum shows respect and sincerity. Relationships tend to form more slowly, but once formed are lasting. Latin America, the Middle East, Asia, and Europe are all formal to one degree or another. The way this formality is shown naturally varies from country to country. Acting familiar with customers from these cultures would not be appropriate.

> Know yourself; know your enemies: One hundred battles, one hundred victories.
> —Sun Tsu,
> *The Art of War*

UNDERSTAND YOUR OWN CULTURAL BACKGROUND

Understanding starts inside your own house. You never leave home without your cultural mindset, your "code of the road," telling you how to behave in social interactions.

To be able to deliver 21st century customer service, you first need to understand and learn about your own cultural lenses. This is not easy to do because you can't really "see" your own biases clearly. It is difficult to distinguish universal human behavior from cultural behavior. You need to keep in mind that what you have always taken for granted as natural and universal is mainly learned cultural behavior.

TECHNIQUE: To start the self-discovery process of your own cultural lenses and the way you do things, think about an experience you have had in another country where there was a cultural clash. How did you feel? What did you do? Whose behaviors did you use to unblock the clash—the ones from home or those of the country you were visiting?

MULTICULTURAL CUSTOMERS

You don't have to leave the U.S. to be international or multicultural. Today your customers can be mainstream Americans, first-generation Americans, second-generation Americans, green-card holders, new arrivals, or international long-term visitors.

With orders coming in over phone and fax lines, through e-mail and the Internet, your customer base could easily extend to most parts of the world. However, the key point to remember is that you don't have to leave the U.S. to be international. The U.S. population today looks like a mini United Nations. Each group brings something to the mix and they are no longer lost in a melting pot. That fact has implications for your customer service.

Minorities Are the Majority

The United States has the fifth largest Hispanic population in the world—about 25 million people.

Your customer service agents could be dealing with as many African-Americans, Arab-Americans, Asian-Americans, Hispanic-Americans, or Indian-Americans as mainstream customers. These groups are gaining in numbers and in purchasing power. The shifting demographics is a serious wake-up call. To grow market share means not to:
- ignore these diverse groups
- lump them into the mainstream
- ignore their unique cultural behaviors, needs, and tastes

Customer service is all about connecting with your customers and building relationships. I always have misgivings about attempting to compress the essence of a society and its culture into a few short phrases. These portrayals could be viewed as perpetuating stereotypes. However, as long as these portrayals or categories are used as the beginning step in the learning process, they can be beneficial.

GETTING TO THE NEW REALITY

Given this new reality, what kind of software filters should you install so that you can:

1. "read" the communication
2. understand the formatting

There are three new hi-tech filters—plus a super filter that will get the first three to work at their maximum potential.

- *Filter 1:* your recognition that the customer from a different cultural background can have different perceptions, beliefs, attitudes, motivation, and philosophy.
- *Filter 2:* your openness to other cultures. There is no good and bad way in the multicultural marketplace—just different ways. Recog- nize this and attempt to make connections with your customer. Only by doing this can you give outstanding customer service.

Using Stereotypes

Develop "stereotypes" only as a way of starting to understand your customers. People normally use such a generalization approach to categorize behaviors as a way of making sense out of what is taking place. If these categories express an "evaluation" or a "judgment" of cultural behavior, they move into the area of prejudice. If they go unrecognized, your customer service can be seriously compromised.

Once you gain more in-depth understanding, it is important to move beyond stereotypes.

Your challenge is to understand but not judge cultural behavior. Remember, there is no good or bad, just different.

• *Filter 3:* your awareness of general cultural behavioral patterns. Your challenge is to discover their "logic" or "rationale"—their cultural drivers—in order to better serve them in the way that best meets their needs.
• *SUPER FILTER:* how to most effectively bridge cultural differences:
  1. Show respect for a customer's behavior.
  2. Show interest in learning about the customer's cultural ways.
  3. Be tolerant of behaviors with which you may not agree.
  4. Gather information in an impartial and nonjudgmental way.

Ready, Set . . .

Now that you are approaching customer service with your new filters, you are ready. By understanding the cultural differences of your customers, you are ready to find ways to accommodate them and give them more dynamic, responsive, and enlightened customer service. You are now prepared to deliver customer service for the 21st century.

BURST INTO ACTION

A journey of 1000 miles starts with the first step.

—Old Chinese saying

Happy journey.

1 List the various cultural backgrounds of your customers.

2 Describe the differences in the way various subgroups of your customers behave. Remember, "culture" can also refer to needs for support,

tendencies to complain, or other service demands.

3 Get your service reps to share their knowledge of different types of customers.

4 Look at the assumptions you make that may bias your behavior.

5 Talk to customers who represent different cultures and find out what you can do for them.

6 Create profiles of different customer types for training purposes.

7 Decide on ways to acknowledge and show respect for customers from each culture.

SECTION III
IMPLEMENTING GREAT SERVICE

USE THE "WHOLE-BRAIN" CUSTOMER SERVICE
SYSTEM TO DELIGHT YOUR CUSTOMERS
Joan E. Cassidy

CREATING A FANATICAL
CUSTOMER SERVICE CULTURE
Peggy Morrow

IMPLEMENTING A QUALITY SERVICE MODEL
Cynthia J. Shaffer

PERSONAL, PROACTIVE SERVICE
THRILLS CUSTOMERS
Rick Crandall

USE THE "WHOLE-BRAIN" CUSTOMER SERVICE SYSTEM TO DELIGHT YOUR CUSTOMERS

Joan E. Cassidy

Joan E. Cassidy, EdD, is one of the America's leading "organizational doctors." She is noted for improving customer satisfaction and increasing productivity and quality as a leader in several private, public, and nonprofit organizations. For the past 25 years, she has helped thousands of managers and their staffs learn the secrets of high performance from both organizational and personal perspectives. She speaks and consults nationally and internationally with *Fortune* 100 and 500 companies, associations, and most Federal government agencies. She has hosted "Integrated Leadership Concepts Presents," a Washington-based cable TV show.

Prior to founding Integrated Leadership Concepts, Inc. in 1992, Dr. Cassidy was an executive with SICPA, Securink, Inc., the primary supplier of security inks for the Bureau of Engraving and Printing. SICPA, a worldwide manufacturing firm, based in Switzerland, supplies ink for 95% of the world's currency. As Director for Total Quality Management, Cassidy established a system based on ISO 9002 and was noted for significantly improving customer and employee satisfaction while reducing scrap and re-work by 300%.

Dr. Joan E. Cassidy, Integrated Leadership Concepts, Inc., P.O. Box 523080, Springfield, VA 22152; phone (703) 866-1184; fax (703) 866-7931; e-mail DrJoanC@aol.com; www.DrJoanCassidy.com.

USE THE "WHOLE-BRAIN" CUSTOMER SERVICE SYSTEM TO DELIGHT YOUR CUSTOMERS

Joan E. Cassidy

> To serve is beautiful, but only if it is done with joy and a whole heart and a free mind.
>
> —Pearl S. Buck

M ost organizations operate with only half a brain! They focus on fiscal and procedural concepts (left-brain) to the detriment of the creative, interpersonal aspects of doing business (right-brain).

What "half brain" companies fail to understand is that people are different. One-size-fits-all policies and procedures don't work. Effective organizations have learned that the only way to consistently delight customers is to integrate both left- and right-brain concepts by using a systematic approach focused on prevention, feedback, and corrective action.

AN UNFORTUNATELY ALL-TOO-TYPICAL CUSTOMER SERVICE EXPERIENCE

Can you remember the worst customer service you ever had and how you felt? Every time I ask this question, without any hesitation whoever I am talking to launches into one or more stories about his or her worst customer service experiences. The stories, besides containing facts, are always laden with emotion. Whether it relates to a defective product, the service received, or both, makes no difference. Most people characterize their experiences in "lose-lose" terms.

In Search of Help for My Ailing Computer

Let me give you a personal example. While I was writing this chapter, my computer started to "lock up" and I would lose whatever I had been working on. It was still under warranty, so I took it back to where I had purchased it. I explained to the technical service representative how critical it was for me to get it back as soon as possible. He said it would take five to seven days. I reluctantly left my computer, giving clear instructions that I wanted a diagnosis and then a phone call before they did anything.

Seven days passed and I had heard nothing. I couldn't get through to the repair department on the phone, so I went back to the store. A very rude customer service clerk informed me that no one had looked at my computer yet. He further told me that the store's "current" policy was seven to ten days and because it had been only seven days, they probably would not get around to it for at least three more days.

Four more days passed (we were now up to eleven days). After an hour's worth of busy signals

"A software conflict? Don't bother isolating the problem. Just erase the hard drive—it takes only seconds and we get $49.97."

and being put on hold three times for over ten minutes each time, I was told that there was nothing wrong with my computer. It was a software problem, so they had reformatted my hard drive. And, because the software was not under warranty, I owed them $49.97!

I was furious. All I had asked for was a diagnosis. Because they reformatted the hard drive, I lost everything that was on it. Fortunately, I had some of the files backed up, but not my most recent files. In addition, I now was faced with the task of reinstalling all of my other software.

Adding Insult to Injury

After I regained my composure, I went to pick up my computer. The person who "assisted" me was even ruder than the one I had encountered the first time. I asked to see the manager and waited for over half an hour before he appeared. When he did, he only repeated the company's policy over and over. It was as though he did not hear a word I said. In frustration, I finally paid the $49.97 (my computer was being held hostage until I paid). Before I left, however, I informed the manager that I would be writing a letter not only to his company, but also to the computer manufacturer and to the software manufacturer. He said that was my prerogative, then turned and walked away without another word.

To make it worse, I was still not sure if it was indeed a software problem. I would have to wait and see if the problem repeated itself. Will I ever buy anything from that store again? *I don't think so!* Have I told numerous people of my experience?

You bet! Does that company need some help with their customer service? *Absolutely!!*

CUSTOMER SERVICE IS WHERE THE RUBBER MEETS THE ROAD

With each interaction, customers or potential customers have positive or negative experiences with your organization. If the experience is positive, both the customer and the organization win. Unfortunately, in many cases, as in the one I described above, customers have such negative experiences they may choose not to do business with that company again. When that happens, both the customer *and* the organization lose, creating a "lose-lose" situation.

World-class organizations understand what it takes to consistently create win-win outcomes that yield delighted customers and higher profits.

Win-Win Service

Smart companies start the service process with the solicitation of ongoing feedback from both their internal and external customers to understand what is going on. They follow through by taking immediate action to correct any discrepancies. Then they set up systems to prevent the same problems in the future.

Other organizations do not practice prevention properly. They have not learned how preventive measures contribute to great customer service, lower costs, and higher profits. Dr. W. Edwards Deming, father of America's quality move-

---

What Do Customers Want?

The American Society for Quality Control asked 1,005 adult consumers what quality factors they considered important when purchasing a product or service. For manufactured items, they wanted performance, durability, ease of repair, service availability, warranty, and ease of use. Price was ranked seventh out of nine factors!

The same survey defined good quality service as courteous, prompt, responding to one's basic needs, and provided by a person with a good attitude. Customers will be more forgiving of difficulites if they perceive that they are being treated with personal care and respect.

—William Band,
Creating Value for Customers

ment, often described the "unknown costs" of poor quality. He urged companies to practice prevention by establishing a systematic approach to how they conducted business.

Others have used the "Factor of 10" to explain the increasing costs of not doing it right the first time. The earlier you detect and fix a problem, the cheaper it is to fix. The further it goes undetected in the process, the more geometrically costly it is to fix. When you consistently practice prevention, you focus on building an error-proof process. Error proofing a process is one of the best ways to guarantee that customers will be delighted every time.

The Factor of 10 Estimate for Costs of Errors

When Correction Is Made During: — *Cost*

- planning — 1¢
- design — 10¢
- manufacturing — $1.00
- after customer receives product or service — $10.00

THE FACTOR OF 10 APPLIED TO CUSTOMER SERVICE

The Factor of 10, originally applied to catching and eliminating defects early in a manufacturing process, has been applied more recently to customer service. When a customer doesn't complain to you directly, that customer will likely tell at least 10 others about the bad experience. Each of those 10 may then tell 10 others and so forth. So you end up having 100, 1,000, or more people hearing about one individual's poor customer service experience!

Feedback and Response

Customer feedback is critical. The problem is, many individuals often go to great lengths to avoid getting negative feedback. If some negative feedback manages to get through, it is either ignored—or worse, the recipient gets defensive, makes excuses, and points his or her finger elsewhere. So, when someone complains to you about poor quality or customer service, don't consider it as an annoyance, but as an opportunity. However, it also must be acted on as quickly as possible. Negative feedback left alone can be devastating.

Any negative feedback is often a signal that something is wrong with either the product quality or with the service someone has received. At minimum, the feedback should be treated as a genuine opportunity to find the source of the problem and fix it before the organization loses customers.

As I work with clients to help them improve the quality of their products and services, we focus on "Whole-Brain Customer Service." We integrate both left- and right-brain concepts to consistently create win-win scenarios by:

- practicing prevention
- continuously seeking internal and external feedback
- finding the source and fixing any problems or potential problems as soon as they are detected

The store in my opening example would benefit from practicing "Whole-Brain Customer Service."

> ### Facts About Complaints
>
> - One in four customers has a problem with products purchased, regardless of whether or not they complain.
> - Twenty-six out of 27 service customers do not complain when things go wrong. For an accurate count of dissatisfied customers, multiply the number of complaints received by 27.
> - A company's profits can be boosted 25–90% from just a 5% decrease in customer-defection rates.
> - Of all positive memories of good service received, fully 25% started out as some kind of failure in service delivery.
>
> —Janelle Barlow and Claus Møller,
> *A Complaint Is a Gift*

A CASE STUDY OF CHANGE

I recently worked with a specific division of a large international manufacturing company to help them build a centralized customer service department. At the time, the company was operating out of three different facilities located in three different states. My client, the Director of Customer Service, was at headquarters, along with other headquarters staff for Finance and Accounting, and Sales and Marketing. Customer Service Representatives (CSRs) were located in two manufacturing facilities, but were somewhat separated from production and quality assurance. Salespeople floated in and out of the three facilities. Furthermore, the company was planning on expanding to other locations.

... lacking good measures, no company can assess its progress or adjust to changes in customer expectations.
—William H. Davidow and Bro Uttal, *Total Customer Service: The Ultimate Weapon*

Establish a Baseline

When I first met with my client, he explained that the company was experiencing customer satisfaction problems. I asked him if they had any data concerning these problems. He admitted that they didn't have any numbers, but there were some anecdotal data. However, he said it would be safe to say that the problems could be grouped into several categories, such as order taking and order processing, product quality, delivery, and invoicing. I asked him to be more specific and he provided these types of examples:

- Marketing and Sales did not follow any consistent procedures for communicating changes, price increases, or other agreements to the Customer Service Representatives, or to the headquarters staff responsible for invoicing.
- Salespeople were constantly making promises that the Customer Service Representatives had difficulty keeping.
- The Customer Service Representatives had to deal with more and more disgruntled customers.
- Inventory control ranged from poor to nonexistent.
- Turnover in warehouse and production staff, plus lack of adequate training, had created problems in product quality.

- Customer Service Representatives varied in how they took and processed orders, providing ample opportunities for mix-ups.
- Dispatch and delivery were handled differently at each plant.
- In general, no consistent written policies and procedures existed for the entire operation.

You Need Realistic Goals

Given the task of turning things around, the Director of Customer Service had set a goal of 100% perfect order completion. I asked him what he meant by "perfect order completion." For example, did he mean that the Customer Service Representatives were expected to take and process 100% of the orders perfectly? Or, did he mean that the customer would be satisfied 100% of the time with the order? He indicated both. He felt that all we needed to do was develop and implement centralized policies, procedures, scripts, and work instructions for the Customer Service Representatives to use as they took orders, entered them into the computer, and dealt with issues that arose later concerning customer orders.

System-Wide Issues

I told him I had strong reservations about their ability to achieve 100% perfect order completion by developing policies, procedures, scripts, and work instructions *only* for the Customer Service Representatives.

When he asked why, I asked him if he had ever heard the phrase, "Garbage in, garbage out?" A rueful smile immediately appeared on his face indicating that he had indeed. At the same time, he explained that the whole organization was working on quality improvement. However, each department was "doing its own thing." He also

> When you aim for perfection, you discover it's a moving target.
> —Anonymous

reminded me that he did not have any control over those other departments. Thus, he felt he could not be responsible for what they did. He ended by saying, "I'm sure you're familiar with how internal politics work in other organizations. Well, we have our fair share of those kinds of issues."

I empathized, but pointed out the inherent weakness associated with trying to improve quality and customer service using a departmentalized as opposed to an integrated whole-brain approach. I briefly explained my integrated Whole-Brain Customer Service Model described later in this chapter, but he admitted he was not sure how we could implement it. He again reiterated his role in the organization and that he was only responsible for Customer Service—meaning taking and processing orders and resolving complaints.

Benefits of Cross-Department Attention to Service

Whirlpool Speciality Products decided that the best way to reduce quality problems was to get production people more involved in customer service. They figured that if these workers heard the complaints directly from the consumers, they would be more determined and better able to make the requested improvements. They were right. Rejected parts dropped from 2,700 per million to 326 per million.

—*Work & Family Newsbrief*

Reality Sets In

Our next session was held in one of the two manufacturing facilities. The purpose of the meeting was for me to get a better sense of how they were currently operating so that I could develop a plan for what needed to be done. However, our agenda was soon scrapped for a more urgent one.

That morning, as the Customer Service Representatives were attempting to take and process orders, they ran into a major problem. They discovered that the plant was unable to fulfill customer orders for that day. In fact, they were 100% overcommitted and needed several days of production just to fill existing orders!

Needless to say, we had just walked into utter

chaos. The Customer Service Representatives were trying to field customer complaints because of late orders while simultaneously trying to take and process new orders. Sales personnel were calling to find out what had happened to *their* customers' orders and were giving the Customer Service Representatives conflicting instructions on how to juggle existing orders.

Finally, as if there already were not enough problems, the plant manager informed us that a major piece of equipment required in the production process had been broken for two weeks and no one had done anything about it. The implication of this latest development? Production would not be able to meet their normal production quota. This would undoubtedly trigger additional complaints about late orders. At that moment, it seemed an impossible situation to almost everyone concerned.

As my client sagged into a chair, he put his hands to his face and moaned, "It's getting worse." After a brief period, he came to grips with the situation. He admitted his original plan would not fix the problems. He further acknowledged that major preventive measures were needed, but many of them were outside of his span of control. We rolled up our sleeves and developed a plan based on "whole-brain" concepts. As this was relatively new to my client, a brief introduction was in order.

> Many companies think they know what quality means in their industry; [but]...it is not those who offer the product, but those whom it serves who have the final word on how well a product fulfills needs and expectations.
> —David Garvin, *Managing Quality*

EARLY WHOLE-BRAIN RESEARCH

The "Whole-Brain" Customer Service Model™ is a proactive approach based on my more than 25 years of experience, first as an employee, then as a manager and executive, and finally as owner of a consulting firm focused on creating high-performance organizations. It is also based on the research conducted by Ned Herrmann and many others.

Herrmann is credited for developing the original whole-brain metaphor. As a young engineer at General Electric, he was charged with finding out why some people were more creative than others. In the process, he discovered Roger Sperry's Nobel Prize-winning split-brain research. And, as they say, "the rest is history."

Early split-brain research conducted in laboratories supplied evidence supporting hemispheric specialization for a variety of tasks. In 1981, Sperry won the Nobel Prize based on these findings. After severing the corpus callosum on a number of subjects, Sperry's team found that the left-brain is usually better at performing logical, analytical, and mathematical tasks, especially if those same tasks involve linear and sequential processing. On the other hand, the right brain seems to be much better at nonverbal, idea formation, intuition, holistic and synthesizing tasks, and activities such as visual and simultaneous processing.

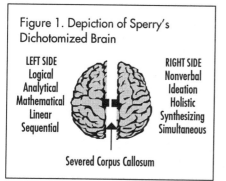

Figure 1. Depiction of Sperry's Dichotomized Brain

LEFT SIDE
Logical
Analytical
Mathematical
Linear
Sequential

RIGHT SIDE
Nonverbal
Ideation
Holistic
Synthesizing
Simultaneous

Severed Corpus Callosum

HERRMANN'S WHOLE-BRAIN MODEL

Since Sperry's discoveries, hundreds of other researchers around the world have developed additional experimental techniques to locate, identify, and measure the degree to which mental capabilities are controlled by one hemisphere or another. A plethora of research now supports a number of different theories about how the brain functions. Some of this research points to the notion that the brain does not operate as simplistically as described originally by Sperry's team.

Ned Herrmann, recognized internationally as the "Father of Brain Dominance Technology," initially used Sperry's left/right dichotomization. He collected data using a forced-choice paper-and-pencil test that he developed at General Electric. However, as his database grew, he noticed that the data did not fit neatly into Sperry's left/right categories. Instead, people were distributed into four distinct categories. In synthesizing his various observations, he developed a metaphorical model of the brain consisting of four quadrants.

Four Mental Preferences

While purely a metaphorical model, Herrmann's four quadrant model has come to be regarded as a valid, reliable measure of mental preferences. Herrmann's four-quadrant model suggests that everyone has a unique mix of thinking and problem-solving modes. However, most people tend to have at least one dominant, or "preferred" mode with a "supporting" secondary mode. Preferences for the remaining modes vary depending on the strength of the primary and secondary modes. In some cases, the least preferred mode may be so weak, it can be characterized as an "avoidance."

The four quadrants consist of left brain or right brain combined with Cerebral or Limbic brain preferences. Cerebral thinkers are usually more comfortable with theories and abstractions, while Limbic thinkers prefer a more pragmatic, hands-on approach. Figure 2 depicts a profile for a person with an upper-left preferred mode, a supporting lower-left mode, a moderate upper-right mode, and an avoidance for the lower-right mode.

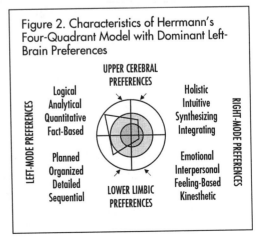

Figure 2. Characteristics of Herrmann's Four-Quadrant Model with Dominant Left-Brain Preferences

UPPER CEREBRAL PREFERENCES

LEFT-MODE PREFERENCES

RIGHT-MODE PREFERENCES

Logical
Analytical
Quantitative
Fact-Based

Holistic
Intuitive
Synthesizing
Integrating

Planned
Organized
Detailed
Sequential

Emotional
Interpersonal
Feeling-Based
Kinesthetic

LOWER LIMBIC PREFERENCES

An avoidance in the lower right can be a red flag, because it may signal communication problems. This usually arises when individuals with different preferences (or avoidances) try to interact.

THE WHOLE-BRAIN CUSTOMER SERVICE MODEL

Research has consistently shown that individuals and teams who integrate and use "whole-brain" concepts are far more successful than those who prefer and use only a "left-brain" or "right-brain" approach. Likewise, a "whole-brain" approach to customer service provides greater results.

After several discussions with my client and others in the organization, we identified the various functions that were in some way linked to customer service. The Whole-Brain Customer Service Model (Figure 3) shows how these functions also are distributed among the four quadrants.

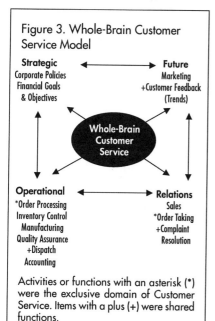

Figure 3. Whole-Brain Customer Service Model

Strategic
Corporate Policies
Financial Goals
& Objectives

Future
Marketing
+Customer Feedback
(Trends)

Whole-Brain Customer Service

Operational
*Order Processing
Inventory Control
Manufacturing
Quality Assurance
+Dispatch
Accounting

Relations
Sales
*Order Taking
+Complaint
Resolution

Activities or functions with an asterisk (*) were the exclusive domain of Customer Service. Items with a plus (+) were shared functions.

PUTTING TOGETHER A SOLUTION

As we proceeded working on the manufacturing firm's customer service, it became evident that 100% perfect orders could not be achieved without dynamic, cross-functional relationships among several departments. In other words, individuals had to tear down their walls and start collaborating. They had to pull together their collective brainpower in order to ensure that customers were 100% satisfied.

In order to create a strong customer service department that would act as a single point of contact for customers from order taking to 100% perfect order completion, we devised a plan based on these three steps:

1. Practice prevention.

2. Continuously seek internal and external feedback.

3. Find the source and fix any problems or potential problems as soon as they are detected.

> It's amazing what you can accomplish if you do not care who gets the credit.
> —Harry Truman

Given the internal politics, I agreed with my client to proceed cautiously to bring the others on board. I have often used these same tactics when I faced similar situations, including when I was Director of Total Quality Management for a large international manufacturing firm. I have also used the same basic model, strategies, and tools in working with other manufacturing companies, the Federal Government, associations, and several service organizations in the technology field.

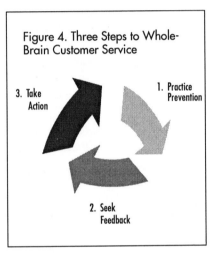

Figure 4. Three Steps to Whole-Brain Customer Service

3. Take Action

1. Practice Prevention

2. Seek Feedback

In other words, it doesn't matter whether you are in manufacturing, service, private, public, or nonprofit organizations. The basics for delivering world-class quality and customer service are the same. Some of the specifics, however, do vary depending on the organization.

Practicing Prevention

I cannot emphasize enough the benefits of practicing prevention. In terms of the bottom line, the benefits were reduced costs and higher profits; for customers, greater satisfaction; for the Cus-

Benefits of Prevention

- reduced costs
- higher profits
- higher customer satisfaction
- fewer hassles
- higher employee satisfaction
- more collaboration among departments

tomer Service Representatives, fewer hassles and more fulfilling work. And, once a plan was in place, other departments began to feel its impact and appreciate the benefits.

A Full Solution

With this approach, my client realized the critical shift that was needed. Up until that point, he had seen his department's role as one of taking and processing orders and then dealing with issues (complaints) from customers concerning those orders. What we put in place were steps to prevent complaints from happening in the first place. Following are some of the immediate strategies and practices we implemented.

- Interviewed CSRs to identify and document how they currently operated.
- Identified macro activities (e.g., order taking, order entry, order processing, claims resolution) and developed flow charts for each of the macro activities. Flagged areas where CSRs differed.
- Met with CSRs to discuss and resolve differences within their areas of responsibility. Met with other departments to resolve issues related to their areas of responsibility.
- Developed policies, procedures, work instructions, forms, checklists, and scripts as appropriate for macro activities.
- Pilot tested and finalized flow charts, policies, procedures, work instructions, forms, checklists, and scripts for macro activities.

- Identified KSAAs (knowledge, skills, abilities, and attitudes) for CSR functions.
- Assessed incumbent CSRs to determine appropriate "fit" for role. Reassigned or released those who did not demonstrate that they had the requisite KSAAs.
- Recruited additional CSRs.
- Conducted training.

Continuously Seeking Internal and External Feedback

In the beginning, my client admitted there was no consistent feedback. Our plan to collect feedback consisted of the types of activities described below.

- Identified categories and sources of exceptions to "Perfect Orders" (e.g., data input errors, pricing inconsistencies, product availability, product quality, dispatch and delivery, inventory control, billing).
- Developed Perfect Order Exception Form for CSRs to use to collect data.
- Established Perfect Order Exception Tracking Database and process to analyze and track data.
- Established regular meetings among the CSRs and individuals (including management levels) from other functions to discuss and resolve issues related to Perfect Order Exceptions.
- On an informal basis discussed satisfaction with customers and, at least once a year, recommended that they conduct a formal customer satisfaction survey.

> . . . a company's most precious asset is its relationship with its customers. It is not who you know, but how you are known to them.
> —Theodore Levitt, *The Marketing Imagination*

Finding and Fixing the Source of Any Problem (or Potential Problem)

Earlier I listed a number of problems that my client described, as well as the chaos that we encountered concerning over-commitment of orders at one of the manufacturing facilities. Needless to say, inventory control was one of the first problems that we decided to fix. Following is a summary of our strategies to fix these and other problems we encountered.

- Developed and implemented a system for Inventory Control.
- Established centralized Customer Service (e.g., all CSRs in one facility; consistent use of CSR manual with flow charts, policies, procedures, work instructions, forms, checklists and scripts; consistent training for CSRs).
- Established pricing database, flow charts, policies, and procedures to ensure that consistent pricing and up-to-date information is available.
- Established levels of authority and responsibility for all functions.
- Established uniform policies and procedures for dispatch.
- Established key accounts and prioritized orders.
- Set ranges for delivery dates.
- Eliminated "surprise" factor for those occasions when the order didn't show up by taking a proactive approach. Notified customers in advance if there were a problem.
- Encouraged Sales Representatives and Customer Service Representatives to up-sell and anticipate needs.

* * * * * *

In brief, a whole-brain system has three simple steps:
1. practice prevention
2. seek continuous feedback
3. continuously improve your system by finding and correcting problems

If you keep focused on these steps, you'll be on your way to world-class customer service.

 ## EXPLODE INTO ACTION

To move the world, we must first move ourselves.

—Socrates

To ensure that your company consistently delights your customers:

1 Use a "whole-brain" approach to set up a complete system that incorporates both procedures and creativity.

2 Set up a method to collect feedback from your service reps.

3 Collect feedback from internal departments that are your customers (those departments to which your deparment provides services).

4 Find the source of potential problems and change your system to prevent them.

5 Practice prevention. Focus 10 times more energy on preventing problems early than on correcting them later.

6 Set up a customer advisory group to get feedback from important customers.

7 Do a broad customer survey.

CREATING A FANATICAL CUSTOMER SERVICE CULTURE

Peggy Morrow

Peggy Morrow, CSP (Certified Speaking Professional), is a speaker, author, consultant, and president of her own training and development firm, Peggy Morrow & Associates. For over 16 years, she has served such clients as NASA, Compaq, Shell, Home Depot, Kroger, The Texas Medical Center, and the U.S. Navy.

She has been a speaker for *Inc.* magazine's "Advanced Customer Service Strategies" conference and has developed comprehensive customer service programs for clients such as the Louisiana Superdome, Cosden Credit Union, Tenet Physician's Healthcare of Louisiana, and many others.

Prior to founding her own company, Mrs. Morrow spent several years as a manager in a department store, working within the areas of customer service and special events. She also shares her expertise as a business columnist who has written over 300 articles on customer service and management and is the author of the book *Customer Service: The Key to Your Competitive Edge.*

Mrs. Morrow has been president of two chapters of the National Speakers Association, and has three times served as a board member of two chapters of the American Society for Training and Development.

Peggy Morrow, Peggy Morrow & Associates, 15810 Brook Forest Drive, Houston, TX 77059; phone (800) 375-1982; fax (281) 286-9477; e-mail pegmorrow@aol.com.

CREATING A FANATICAL CUSTOMER SERVICE CULTURE

Peggy Morrow

The people who truly get things done are monoma-
niacs. They focus intensely on one thing at a time.
—Peter Drucker

Have you heard the story about the Nordstrom store in Alaska that let a customer return tires, even though Nordstrom doesn't sell tires? Or the one about the consultant who boarded the plane on his way to an important meeting and realized he had left his dress shoes at home? He called Nordstrom from the airport to get the store to stay open longer so he could get there between flights. But instead, the clerk got his size and style preference and took a taxi with ten pairs of shoes to the airport to be sure the customer would make his connecting flight.

Or the time a Nordstrom store didn't do the suit modifications on time and Fedexed them to the hotel in time for use?

Or the customer who left her plane ticket on the Nordstrom counter and the clerk brought it to the airport in time for the flight?

Or the clerk who delivered something to the customer's home to make up for a delay?

Or the fact that Nordstrom was rated the best department store by customers in a city that didn't have a Nordstrom store?

The point is, there are a lot of stories about great service at Nordstrom that are circulated and recirculated by thrilled customers. Nordstrom knows that providing superb service is the most cost-effective marketing they can do, no matter what it costs them.

Nordstrom Wants Customers to Tell Tales

Stories create legends and free word-of-mouth advertising that is much more powerful than any traditional media. The stories are so powerful that people pass the word on their own so that others around the country hear the stories even if they've never been to a Nordstrom store.

Nordstrom has created one of the best customer service reputations in the country. They are fanatical about it.

Great customer service programs only work when you are fanatical about serving the customer. Any organization can issue

---

Full Service Sells

Sheldon Bowles is an entrepreneur from Canada who, in the 1970s, when everyone was going to self-service gas stations, decided to go to full service. He created a series of gas stations across Western Canada called Domo Gas.

Sheldon's vision of perfection was that going to one of his stations would be like an Indianapolis 500 pit stop. All the attendants, dressed in red jumpsuits, would race to your car when you drove in. One would begin under your hood, one would pump gas, while yet another would ask you to step out of the car, offer you a cup of coffee and a newspaper, and then "dustbust" your car.

Sheldon's stations blew away the competition. They created raving fans. Raving fans are customers who are so excited about what you do that they want to brag about you. They become part of your sales force.

—Ken Blanchard

a few policies about how important customers are and set up a reasonable-sounding program. But, if that were all there was to it, we, as customers, would all be thrilled by service a lot more than we are. If the entire organization doesn't point toward customers and acknowledge them as the purpose of their whole process, you cannot hope to deliver top quality customer service.

Yes, the interpersonal skills and professional image of frontline employees are critical for success. But if you believe that training in these skills alone can guarantee the success of a customer service program, you are setting yourself up for failure.

You need to set up a true customer service culture. Culture involves unwritten standards or norms of behavior—the ways that people act and are expected to act. It also involves a set of shared values—the most important concerns and goals shared by people in the company. A corporate culture that doesn't place a high value on customer service and does not include shared values and norms of behavior will ruin any attempt to improve customer service.

> When aligned around shared values, and united in a common purpose, ordinary people accomplish extraordinary things.
> —Ken Blanchard and Michael O'Connor, *Managing by Values*

DEVELOPING A CUSTOMER SERVICE CULTURE

So how do you go about changing a company's culture to one of fanatical devotion to the customers? I organize the process into eight steps:

- create a vision
- walk the talk
- insist on getting customer feedback
- set clear standards and measure them
- recognize and reward performance
- make your policies customer friendly
- empower and train employees
- remove those who don't fit a customer-oriented culture

Following are some guidelines for how you can implement each stage of this process.

Create a Vision

Without a shared vision of the great service that customers should receive, efforts to improve service delivery will dissolve into confusing, time-consuming projects and initiatives going in different directions—or nowhere at all. When you share a vision of what customer service should be, your employees will be able to act on their own, because they will know the level of commitment to customers that you support.

For instance, do you want your company to be so well known for its top-notch service that customer service becomes a competitive weapon—or will you settle for somewhere in the middle of the pack? Are you going to compete strictly on providing the lowest price, or are you going to add value through service?

A vision statement of a department store chain states: "We want our customers to view us as providing more than just acceptable service. Our goal is to provide legendary service in every shopping experience."

A vision is important for three reasons:

1. A vision clarifies the direction that the company is taking. A vision says "This is where we are going." When everyone knows where they are going, a common culture develops.

2. A vision helps motivate people to take action that is not necessarily in their short-

---

4 Attributes of a Powerful Vision

An effective vision for leading change:

1. conveys a realistic but ambitious goal to force people out of their comfortable routines.

2. must be clear enough to guide decision making so that each employee can look to the vision for how to act in specific situations.

3 must be flexible enough to allow individual initiative as well as adjustments to changing circumstances.

4. must be easy to explain—if you can't explain your vision in less than five minutes, then the vision is unfocused, or worse, uncompelling.

—John Kotter, *Leading Change*

> Without vision, the
> people perish.
> —The Bible

> The very essence of
> leadership is you
> have to have a
> vision. It's got to be
> a vision you
> articulate forcefully
> on every occasion.
> You can't blow an
> uncertain trumpet.
> —Rev. Theodore
> Hesburgh

term interests. New programs and ways of doing things will take people out of their comfort zones by requiring them to do things differently. A credit union client of mine is giving his employees new titles of "service consultants." They are now responsible for knowing much more about their products and the benefits of each. Their new role is a whole lot different from the simple "order takers" and tellers that they were before. The manager of the credit union has a strong vision of improved member service. He's constantly reminding everyone of this vision and is working to expand employees' comfort zones to get them there.

3. A vision helps to coordinate action. If everybody knows where you are headed, they can make decisions and take action without constantly checking with their boss or peers. Without a shared sense of vision, people will be unsure of what action to take.

Once you have established your vision, you must repeat, repeat, repeat it. Have executives find three or four opportunities a day to tie conversations into the vision. Listen to everyone's feedback on the vision and the best way to get there. Your vision must be communicated often and through many channels.

Focus on Specifics

An exercise that I often use is for everyone from the bottom to the top to write down how what they do contributes to the vision. This helps everyone see that his or her particular job is important to making the vision happen. It also makes the vision come "alive," rather than just being a bunch of words on a wall plaque.

Another client of mine has a contest once a month at random intervals. He roams the halls of his business and awards shiny, new silver dollars to anyone who can recite the vision from memory.

You can't just roll a vision out and expect people to buy into it. It must be repeated again and again—on posters, mugs, in meetings and other communication channels. In your company newsletter, feature lots of "hero stories" of employees who have done an extraordinary job in customer service so people get the idea that this behavior is rewarded. When the same message is heard at least six different ways, it will begin to take root in your culture.

Walk the Talk

Management must lead the way and model the service vision. If you do the opposite of what you say, no one will listen to you. The enthusiasm of your employees reflects that of the manager. Your staff will take their cue on how to treat the customer from those higher up on the ladder.

"Ho, ho, ho, to get a refund, just fill out these 12 forms in purple ink, get them notarized, yuk-yuk, and bring them back here by 7 a.m. tomorrow, hee-hee-hee."

I once observed a department store manager being nasty to a customer about a return. Yet all around the employee areas were "The customer comes first" signs. This manager was obviously setting the wrong example. How do you think his employees will act the next time a customer returns an item? A deeply embedded customer service culture comes from what you do, not what you say.

One of my clients, Home Depot, is very good about indoctrinating everyone from the top down in the culture of the importance of the customer. I once saw a group of high-level executives stop their tour of a retail store to ask an obviously befuddled customer, "Are you finding everything you need?" The executive then went to find what the customer wanted. What a great example of walking the talk! That kind of behavior reinforces the vision of customer service that Home Depot has established—that the customer always comes first, even over the time of important executives.

Will Rogers said, "People learn from observation, not conversation." The chairman of a department store in Texas knows this. That's why he walks up and down six flights of stairs during the busy lunch hours so that he will not take up space on an elevator that could be used by a customer. Does this send a strong message about the philosophy of service to his frontline employees who are actually serving the customer? You bet it does!

Look around. Are some of the people in your organization giving only lip service to your vision? Norman Vincent Peale once said, "There is nothing more confusing than people who give good advice but set bad examples." Part of management commitment to a customer service vision and strategy is to act as the ultimate role model. You must "think customer" in everything that you do.

Be Fanatical About Getting Customer Feedback

Your whole organization should be tuned into the voice of the customer. There must be several methods in place to get feedback from your customers on how well you are doing. When the voice of the customer permeates your company, it is easy to establish a culture of customer service.

To hear your customers, you must do everything you can to get to know them and to understand what they want. Then focus the whole company in that direction. Don't assume that you know what they want.

Homebuilder Kaufman & Broad assumed that their Denver customers loved snuggling up in front of a fire on a snowy winter evening. That's why fireplaces were standard in all the homes K&B

Be like the company that keeps one chair empty at all management meetings. The chair is for the customer who should have a say in all policy decisions.

—John Schuster, Hum-Drum to Hot-Diggity

built there. Then they decided to test that assumption by asking potential home buyers what they actually wanted in a house. Surprise! Half the survey respondents said they would willingly forgo a fireplace if it meant they could shave $2000 off the price of the house. So K&B no longer offers them as standard features there.

A print shop client has signs posted all over the shop saying "Is it good enough? Ask the customer." They constantly poll their customers through surveys and face-to-face interviews to see how they are doing and consequently adjust their services to reflect that feedback.

Use some of these methods to listen to your customers.

1. Focus groups. Small groups of your customers you gather together and ask about problems or expectations of your service.

2. Questionnaires. Make them short, easy to answer, and reward customers in some way when they complete them.

3. Telephone surveys. They give you more flexibility in your questions because you can change the direction of the survey depending on the answers of your customers.

4. Frontline to management communication. Collect data and get customers' comments back to management on a regular basis. This technique is especially effective in establishing a culture of service.

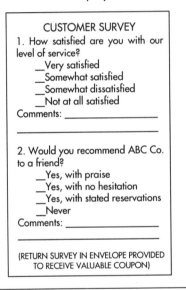

Customer Feedback Forms

Design your forms so that customers can quickly check off their ratings, but provide space for more in-depth comments.

Standard areas of measurement include overall satisfaction with the service received, would the customer recommend your organization, would the customer return, and ratings of their interactions with employees.

CUSTOMER SURVEY

1. How satisfied are you with our level of service?
   __Very satisfied
   __Somewhat satisfied
   __Somewhat dissatisfied
   __Not at all satisfied
Comments: _____
_____

2. Would you recommend ABC Co. to a friend?
   __Yes, with praise
   __Yes, with no hesitation
   __Yes, with stated reservations
   __Never
Comments: _____
_____

(RETURN SURVEY IN ENVELOPE PROVIDED TO RECEIVE VALUABLE COUPON)

5. Face-to-face personal interviews. This is one of the simplest ways to get customer feedback. Everyone in the company should be involved in interviewing customers for their opinions on the level of service your company offers. Let executives work behind the counter as cosmetic giant Estée Lauder does. Send frontline representatives out to your customer's places of business to find out what they like and don't like about your service.

6. Customer panel discussions. Gather a group of your customers together and let all your employees observe a facilitated panel discussion by these customers. There is no more powerful way to hear the voice of your customer than to see them right in front of you talking about what is good and bad about your service.

More Ways to Listen to Customers

- mystery shoppers (see Chapter 4)
- 800 number hotline
- call one customer a day just to say hello
- on your Web site (see Chapter 6)
- observe or videotape customer interactions
- customer advisory councils

Set Standards, Then Measure Your Performance

Setting specific service standards and then measuring your success against them is very important in establishing a culture of service in your organization. It provides a goal toward which all people on your team can aim. Making your goal improved service will give everyone a strong message that service matters.

The process of setting service standards lets everyone, from the top down, know who is responsible for what jobs. It also lets everyone on the team know exactly what they must do to provide superior customer service.

Standards can be developed from customer feedback. Do customers complain about the phone not being answered in a timely fashion? Set some goals that will satisfy them, measure how well you

> If you don't know where you're going, any path will take you there if you walk long enough.
> —The Cheshire Cat to Alice in *Alice in Wonderland*

are doing, and then reward people when they achieve the targets.

Avoid service standards that are not observable, clear, concise and realistic. If your standards are intangible, you won't be able to measure your progress.

All employees including top executives should be measured and evaluated against customer satisfaction ratings and standards. In fact, it is very important to the establishment of a customer service culture that top managers' pay be tied to customer satisfaction.

> ## Some Examples of Service Standards
>
> - All telephone calls will be returned within 24 hours.
> - All merchandise will be shipped within two days.
> - Telephones will be answered before the fourth ring.
> - Treat internal customers with the same courtesy and respect as external customers.
> - 95% on-time, done-right-the-first-time installations.

Recognize and Reward

It's a well known fact that you get more of what you reward. Most employees want proof that their efforts are leading somewhere. Don't make the mistake of only rewarding people once or twice a year. To create a culture of service, employees need lots of short-term wins. (See also Chapter 3.)

Have a regular program to reward for increments of the desired behavior. Target a few "low hanging apples" or easy-to-achieve goals in customer service and then celebrate like crazy when people achieve them.

Short-term wins also undermine naysayers and resisters to the new culture of service. They can serve as a powerful motivator to "get on board." But don't

>
>
> ## Aim High
>
> Challenging goals are often more engaging, effective, and positively energizing than merely "high" goals. When organizations go for 6 Sigma quality (defined as only a few errors per million), it is a real challenge.
>
> For example, when President Kennedy said we'd put men on the moon and return them safely, it engaged the country's imagination at a time when the U.S. was behind the Russians in terms of our space program.
>
> Involve all employees in setting service standards. They will often define far higher goals than managers will.

Recognition Ideas

Here are just a few ideas for rewards and recognition besides money.

- "Gone fishin" certificate. This allows employees to leave work 30 minutes early on a day of their choice.
- "Sleep in" certificate. Allows employees to choose any day they would like to come to work 30 minutes late.
- WOW awards (Wonderful, Outstanding Work). When employees go the extra mile, like staying late to meet a deadline for a customer, they receive a "WOW Gram" that is posted on the bulletin board and a blue marble that goes into a glass jar on their desks. Ten blue marbles gives the employee a gold marble plus a T-shirt embroidered with "WOW" and the company logo. Gold marbles earn bigger prizes.
- Fun, quick recognitions like awarding a potholder for handling of a "hot" (demanding) customer with extreme diplomacy and tact, an egg timer for the best quick decision, and a wacky "stress hat" for the person who had the most stressful customer that week.
- "Trading Places" day. Senior executives spend an hour answering phones or serving customers while customer reps supervise them.

make the mistake of sending the message that "you can relax now, we've met our goal." People will lose their sense of urgency and reduce their efforts. Once you've achieved a goal, quickly set a new target at which to take aim.

Make sure that people are rewarded for the desired behaviors. If your employees look around and see that speed is recognized more than making the customer happy, guess what will happen?

This is a fault of many call centers. Customer service representatives are judged on how many calls they handle per hour rather than how satisfied the customers are with those calls. It's easier to measure the length of the call than customer satisfaction, but in the end speed will only get you unhappy customers.

Reward and recognition programs succeed when you keep rewards visible and never give them unless they are earned. Avoid "Employee of the Month" programs unless you are sure that they will not become "pass around" awards, where everyone gets a turn. There should be some strict criteria from both peers and managers to determine the award.

One of the most powerful forms of recognition is simply to treat your employees with respect. Listen to their ideas and value their opinions. By doing so, you show them that they are important members of the customer service team. This simple action is a major motivator and will go a long way toward establishing a culture of service in your organization.

Say Yes to Customers

At L.L. Bean, the rule is that you have to get permission to say no to the customer, rather than permission to say yes! Think what a difference that policy makes!

Make All Policies Customer-Friendly

You must care so much about your customers that your processes and procedures can be twisted to meet their needs instead of the other way around. Whenever there is a question of which way to do something, the company with a deeply-ingrained customer service culture will choose the way that is easiest for the customer, even if it costs a little more.

I recently worked with a company where all the policies in their accounts receivable department were designed for the convenience of the company. The customer had to submit things in exactly the form that the company wanted. Forget that it didn't work with the customer's method of doing business. Is it any wonder that they had many unhappy customers?

Another company has a monthly "What's stupid, what's customer unfriendly?" meeting to weed out practices that work against their culture of customer service.

Be ruthless about getting rid of polices and procedures that make it hard for your customer to do business with you. Those policies will send the message that your company is more important than the customer, which will quickly erode your efforts to establish a culture of service.

Empower and Train Employees

Empowerment is self-direction, helping people to take responsibility, and giving them the authority to make decisions that affect their customers. Empowerment permits speed in decision making, allows people to collaborate freely, and promotes the cultivation of creativity and quality.

If your vision of great customer service is going to work, employees must be given a high level of decision-making power where the customer is concerned. Every employee should be asked to assume personal responsibility for achieving superior customer service. This will avoid the "having to ask the boss" if you can give $25.00 more dollars of merchandise back to a disgruntled customer or "comp" the meal of an unhappy diner.

In an internal customer service situation, empowerment gives the employee the authority to ask people who use a form on a regular basis to suggest improvements and modify the form before it is reprinted.

Employees must feel free to take the lead in rectifying any less-than-perfect situation. This can include sending the customer a letter of apology or explanation, or, if appropriate, a bouquet of flowers.

Of course there must be parameters. Some people will try to "give away the store" unless guided. Determine just how far you will feel comfortable letting them go. For instance, you could say that they are empowered to spend up to $250 to solve the problem and if it goes over that, to check with a manager. But

Empowerment and Feedback Is a Fragile Process

Situations and problems you have not anticipated are guaranteed to arise. Sometimes employees may not handle the situation as you would have liked. But remember, employees are the ones who are there making a decision while dealing with the stress of the moment.

If an employee has gone overboard in satisfying a customer, take it easy on the employee. First, congratulate the employee on making the customer happy. Stress that this is your primary goal and that you are happy that the employee accomplished it. Then you can suggest alternatives the employee might try the next time this situation occurs (for example, offering a restaurant patron who is only slightly dissatisfied with her meal complimentary beverages for the table rather than comping the entire meal).

To make sure the employee does not feel that this feedback is a reprimand, again praise the employee for his or her taking the initiative in keeping the customer happy.

push your limits on this, because you will find that employees will not usually go overboard.

Training, Training, Training. Saying "Poof—you're empowered" doesn't work. Employees need to understand exactly what that means and receive the training that will allow them to do it.

Give your employees constant, intensive, and universal training in customer care. This will also help establish a shared culture of customer service excellence. Your people will not magically know how to handle a difficult, screaming customer, for instance. Give them the skills to do it.

Don't make the mistake of thinking that training in customer service is only for the frontline people. In order for a culture of service to take root, everyone from the top down must have training.

Of course it won't all be the same training. Administration and executives should be trained in skills and strategies needed in establishing and reinforcing the culture. Managers and supervisors need training in how to make the customer service process a reality and forge a team which is all working toward the same service goals.

> **Keep a Customer Service Scrapbook**
>
> Keep a scrapbook or database of customer service problems and how they were solved. Have employees write up these problem-solution scenarios at the end of each day.
>
> When other employees read the stories, they will be alerted to scenarios that might arise with another customer. In addition, it will become a valuable training guide for new employees.

Frontline customer contact people need to learn the skills, behaviors, and attitudes for dealing with customers. Everyone else in the company should be trained in customer service awareness and internal customer service. Only then will a service culture be in place.

Remove Those Who Don't Fit the Culture

Working with customers—both internal and external—is a tough, emotional job. Not everyone will be good at it. Too many companies allow frontline service representatives or people who deal with internal customers to remain on the job when they are not suited to a customer service position.

You must quickly weed out those who cannot, or will not, support the customer-centered culture of the company. If employees do not want to serve their customers in the best way possible, document their behaviors and use this information to help them change or to move them to areas away from customer interaction. One of the strongest messages you can give about the importance of customer service in your organization is to terminate those employees who are not customer focused.

If you allow people who are doing it "wrong" to continue to be employed, or to stay in service positions, you will quickly infect all the others who are doing it right. They will develop a "who cares" attitude and customer satisfaction will soon head downhill.

Even before your people are hired, they pick up on the culture of your company. Even if they came on board totally committed to customer service, when a company's culture does not live, sleep, eat, and breathe the message that the customer comes first, the new employees will model the behavior that they see around them. That is why establishing a culture of being fanatical about the customer is so important.

> Being friendly is necessary, but friendliness alone does not constitute excellent service. People skills require that employees be well trained in their jobs, confident, communicative, reliable, courteous, credible, energetic, knowledgeable, attentive, and caring, with an attitude of "I can do it for you now."
> —Michael E. Cafferky, *Let Your Customers Do the Talking*

SUMMARY

Changing your culture to reflect an emphasis on the customer requires both strong, consistent action and patience. It will not and cannot happen overnight. You need to actively encourage people to accept the new culture and have the patience to give the culture time to become ingrained.

A culture can't be changed by a series of training classes or a simple memo from the president that "We will now become more customer friendly." Catchy slogans on the wall and on coffee mugs are only reinforcement for changing a culture. You must be fanatic about providing the customer with exceptional service.

BURST INTO ACTION

Success seems to be connected with action. Successful people keep moving. They make mistakes, but they don't quit.

—Conrad Hilton

1 Agree on a brief vision statement about service of 50 words or less, and preferably 20 words or less.

2 Gather stories of great service from your organization and circulate them.

3 Have each employee write down how they contribute to the vision.

4 Set up one or more regular customer feedback mechanisms.

5 Include at least one face-to-face session with customers.

6 Set specific, high goals for service.

7 Set up one small and one large reward program for great service.

8 Reward people for finding customer-unfriendly procedures.

Chapter 10

IMPLEMENTING A QUALITY SERVICE MODEL

Cynthia J. Shaffer

Cindy Shaffer
is the president and CEO of
Create Solutions, Inc., a management and online solutions
firm. Create Solutions specializes in the design and development of customer-
focused, quality initiatives. Ms. Shaffer founded the organization in January of
1997 after 20 years of customer service experience gained by working through
the ranks of numerous organizations and roles of responsibility.

The firm offers customized consulting and training services. Consulting
expertise includes: call center design and development, customer service and
quality re-engineering, Internet solutions (consulting and development), Year 2000
projects, and QuickBooks Financial software implementations and support.
Some of her clients include AT&T, Kinetic Concepts, and American Outfitters.

Ms. Shaffer is a graduate of Florida Southern College with a BS degree in
Business Management. She is a member of numerous trade organizations and
community leadership positions including various Who's Who distinctions.

She attributes much of her success to her ability to communicate and relate
to people at all levels of an organization and her ability to negotiate the Win!
Win! Win!

Cindy Shaffer, Create Solutions, Inc., 1404 Ridgeview Drive, Somerset, PA 15501;
phone (814) 445-9077; fax (814) 443-9806; e-mail cshaffer@
createsolutions.com or cshaffer@somersetcounty.com.

IMPLEMENTING A QUALITY SERVICE MODEL

Cindy Shaffer

Quality is not an action, it is a habit.

—Aristotle

Each of the chapters in this book has provided ideas on how you can improve your customer service.

But, in order to create a great service culture, you have to implement a specific program where one-to-one, personal service becomes a habit. Quality programs have often been successful in the past because they bring a complete system of implementation to bear. Here's an example.

Company X had always had good service and many loyal customers. Their business was stable and profitable. A mid-level company executive, Sue, went to a workshop on quality customer service. At the beginning of the workshop, the instructor asked attendees to write down their companies' customer satisfaction ratings for the last three years and to give two examples of extraordinary service their company had provided customers. Sue couldn't think of any great stories and knew she didn't have any data.

The workshop inspired Sue to start documenting service levels. When she talked to executives back at her company, they all could give examples of a couple of long-term customers. But they had no specific examples of great service stories. They told Sue that the company's customer service was fine, but if she wanted to spend a little time on the side documenting it, that would be okay.

When Sue talked to frontline reps, she got a few examples of very good service, but more comments about cases where reps felt blocked by bureaucracy or "company policy" from doing anything out of the ordinary for customers.

> Business is built on the loyal customer, one who comes back and brings a friend.
> —W. Edwards Deming

What Customers Said

When Sue called the company's dozen biggest customers, she got a serious shock. In several cases, the contact name in the database was gone. In one case, even the phone number was bad. In two cases, people told her they were glad she'd called because they had a problem with something and hadn't gotten around to calling the company. In both of these cases, they said they didn't know exactly who to talk with anyway. The rest of the customers said everything was okay, but couldn't offer any stories of Company X's great service.

Sue realized that the picture was worse than it looked. The twelve biggest customers who were used as references were not up to date in the database. Two of them were unhappy about something and the rest were passive. Not one customer could give her a story of great service.

Implementing Change

The full story of what Sue did over the next three years is too long to tell here. She started enlisting support from both upper management and frontline reps for her team. At first, people just went along as a favor. They didn't really see what the problem was.

Among the early steps Sue was able to take were:

- creating a customer satisfaction survey and seeing that it was used regularly
- creating a customer advisory board that met once a quarter
- assigning specific people to each of the 20 biggest customers—one frontline rep and one in top management
- starting a policy of assigned contacts "checking in" with their major customers—just to keep in touch
- starting an e-mail newsletter that went out to customers, prospects, and employees and shared stories of great service

At the end of three years, Sue's company had a real quality service program in place, support from consultants, customer ratings were way up, and Sue had been promoted—twice.

QUALITY
SERVICE STEPS

1. Survey customers
2. Create advisory board
3. Assign contacts to big customers
4. Check in regularly

WHAT TQM IS—AND ISN'T

Much of my work has come from a Total Quality Management (TQM) perspective, as does this chapter. However, the "image" of TQM in many people's minds is wrong. Many people think of the Total Quality movement as an older "fad" that focuses on precise statistical measurement of tiny incremental improvements (SPC—statistical process control).

Few people realize that the implementation of ISO registrations and other quality initiatives is still growing. Even fewer people know that *customer service* is the major quality criterion for total quality. For instance, when you look at the guidelines for ISO certification, the majority revolve around documenting systems for gathering customer input. Or, as Philip Crosby put it in *Quality Without Tears* where he amplifies Deming's concepts, "Quality is defined as conformance to customer requirements. It is not a matter of opinion or a measure of 'goodness' [of products]."

WHY WORRY ABOUT QUALITY SERVICE ?

Customers no longer have to settle for a functional product, a competitive price, and good service. Today, customers can command quality products, the best prices, and *great* customer service. Customers expect it as a starting point. You must now differentiate yourself through new and creative means. You must provide more value than competitors.

What Is ISO Certification?

ISO-9000, 14000, etc. is a system of standards developed by the International Organization for Standardization (ISO). Started in Europe, the standards are accepted by more than 50 countries.

Certification for service businesses is also available. For example, for a office machine repair business, a few of the customer service attributes that might be measured are:

• machine fixed right the first time
• promptness of service
• courtesy of service rep
• telling client what was fixed
• work area left clean

Service Now Recognized as Key

When top quality and good prices are a given in a market, your key to success must revolve around your people delivering great service. The role that customer service professionals now play has brought them to the forefront of attention.

As the key players in delivering quality service, customer service professionals can create and capitalize on competitive advantages for their organizations. The main tool that customer service professionals need to deliver great customer service is a successful *quality service model*. This model is the key to making today's competitive game a quality experience for all of the players (customer, organization, and customer service rep [CSR]).

The focus of this chapter will be to show you how to develop and implement a Win! Win! Win! strategy for the customer, the organization, and the CSR. This will be based on a simple 4-Ts model called Successful Quality Service.

Quality Customer Service Is Key

What prevents all companies from meeting the quality service challenge head on? The answer is simple. Most companies don't know how!

Businesses planned for service are apt to succeed; businesses planned for profit are apt to fail.
—Nicholas M. Butler

Companies traditionally have competed on product, price, or service. In the past, market leadership has been determined largely in the product or price arenas by name-brand products or cutthroat pricing. Most organizations have been successful—and maintained their comfort levels—by competing in delivering tangibles to their customers. However, they are inexperienced and very uncomfortable when it comes to competing in the intangible service arena.

Unfortunately for these service laggards, the intangible aspects of service are no longer discretionary. Survivors of the competitive pressures must immediately shift gears and change priorities to *customer-focused service* because:

(1) Competitors *can* quickly and easily duplicate quality products and competitive prices. This will undermine short-term successes based on quality and price and lead to long-term failures.

(2) Competitors *can not* duplicate human resources! Collectively, people drive all

aspects of quality, especially in the service arena. Competitive companies have learned to capitalize on this fact and effectively leverage existing human resources as their secret weapon for sustained, long-term growth.

What Should You Do?

Any person or process that the customer interacts with directly should be the first to be re-engineered by a quality change program. These areas of the business can produce the quickest and most significant changes in the way your customer perceives your business.

By focusing on customer interactions, immediate results will be recognized in cost reductions, increased productivity, increased sales, and dramatically improved customer survey results (from both internal and external customers). The expertise of customer service professionals makes and breaks organizations.

Dispense with the hierarchy and send in the teams! One of the pioneers and best examples of companies that have successfully deployed customer quality models is General Electric. By removing their hierarchy, this industry giant has created over 100 teams that lead their organization.

General Electric's CEO, Jack Welch, cites the GE effort to deploy a Quality Service Model as hugely successful in an article in *USA Today.* Here's his assess-

---

GE's Model: "Finding a Better Way Every Day"

Here are GE CEO Jack Welch's tips to success:

- Have a passion for excellence and hate bureaucracy.
- Be open to ideas from anywhere.
- Live quality . . . and drive cost and speed for competitive advantage.
- Have the self-confidence to involve everyone and behave in a boundaryless fashion.
- Create a clear, simple, reality-based vision.
- Have enormous energy and the ability to energize others.
- Stretch . . . set aggressive goals . . . reward progress . . . yet understand accountability and commitment.
- See change as an opportunity— not a threat.
- Have global brains . . . and build diverse and global teams.

ment on the role service played in their efforts so far and his prediction as to the role it will play in the future of GE:

> Service is so great an opportunity . . . that our vision for the next century is that GE be recognized as a global *service company* that also sells high-quality products.

USE THE 4 Ts TO BUILD A SUCCESSFUL QUALITY SERVICE MODEL

Developing the Win! Win! Win!

This all sounds good, but how do you do it? How do you overcome the reluctance to embrace change that occurs as a natural defense by most people?

Organizations that want to survive this service-quality revolution must respond by effectively leveraging the four Ts :

- *Teamwork*
- *Training*
- *Technology*
- *Trust*

These four Ts are the key entities in our model. The key to getting the "buy-in" that you need to enact the model lies in negotiating benefits for all of the parties—make it fun and productive! The key to developing the Win! Win! Win! is to have all parties actively involved in the establishment of goals, the execution of the model, and, most importantly, participating in the rewards of the win.

Getting started in the process requires, first, a firm commitment from all levels of management that a change is in order. Second, the team must agree to a new culture that "walks the talk" of a customer-focused organization. The new role of leadership in this model shifts. Team dynamics can be threatening to leaders because appearances might mislead them into perceiving there are no longer roles for their expertise.

Teamwork

Teams are the most effective way to leverage all resources because they are a powerful structure in maximizing each player's strengths and minimizing the individual's weaknesses.

Team dynamics is also the critical driver in changing customer perceptions. Effectively managed team dynamics shift customer perceptions of a company from reactive to proactive overnight. Before the team structure is implemented, it is critical that the organization assesses the most effective type of team and a comfortable level of decision-making authority to empower them.

There are several types of teams: process or project, functional or cross-functional, and also varying authority levels: self-directed or semiautonomous. The goals and culture of the organization, its market, and its customer base are all things to consider before you choose the team structure and authority levels that are best for your organization.

L.L. Bean is a great example in the retail arena of superb customer service. What customers don't see directly is the team dynamics that support this outstanding customer service.

Tips for Successful Team Dynamics

1. Involve everyone in determining the type of team structure, the authority levels and the goals. If you do not get buy-in on these fundamental issues, it is likely that change will be slow and unsuccessful.

2. Management needs to "walk the talk." The biggest risk to success in implementing team dynamics is to superimpose a team model on top of a firmly existing hierarchy.

3. Make the changes in a logical order at a pace with which all the players feel comfortable. It is healthy to set aggressive goals, but it can be risky to move forward without allowing the team to gain confidence in the changes.

4. Reward the wins! It is critical that the team takes time to celebrate when goals are met. Regardless of whether the wins are small or large, a great amount of support for the initiative and momentum for the team will be gained by sharing the wins with the players. This is not only true during the implementation but should also be employed as an ongoing change agent. (See also Chapter 3.)

I am tough when it comes to giving world-class ratings to companies in customer service, but L.L. Bean has reached that distinction in my mind because quality service is not an occasional thing. It's a daily practice! My perception of L.L. Bean is a company that provides world-class, quality service, each and every time.

If you haven't ever shopped with L.L. Bean, you are missing something. What makes them so great? With L.L. Bean, the customer is truly "king." L.L. Bean employees are knowledgeable not only in a reactive sense, but are also proactive. When I call L.L. Bean, I'm always impressed. They know my previous buying history, my preferences, my sizes, and my key information. In fact, when I call, they even know it's me. One of the keys to this overall quality experience lies in the service model that L.L. Bean has deployed with their team structure.

> A team is a small number of people with complementary skills who are committed to a common purpose, performance goals, and an approach for which they hold themselves mutually accountable.
> — Jon R. Katzenbach and Douglas K. Smith, *The Wisdom of Teams*

Training

How can your customer service professionals execute their service techniques in the same successful fashion as an L.L. Bean professional? The answer is that the company and individuals must have a commitment to training. Investing in training for your customer service professionals is essential. Most companies estimate that every dollar invested in training returns five to fifteen dollars in benefits.

In the eyes of the customer, all of your organization's professionals should be well trained and proactive. The value of well-trained versus untrained or casually-trained professionals is the difference between great and good customer service! The polish that training provides enhances the customer's experience of the service you deliver. Remember, you are preparing these professionals to drive your company image and positive customer perceptions.

In order to determine the types and quantities of training, it is important to do individual skills assessments and tailor the training to meet the needs of the individuals. Once the training is complete, encourage and empower problem solving at all levels.

One opportunity to differentiate your customer service from competitors is to have individuals who specialize in key customer areas (for example, by customer, by product, geographic location, or by process).

Training is how a company reproduces its standards and culture. World-class service organizations have individuals empowered and trained to convert customer problems into customer opportunities. Train your team to rise to the occasion.

> ## Getting the Most Out of Your Training Dollars
>
> Motorola claims to have gotten a 3300% return on their training dollars—when managers supported the training and made sure employees used their new skills. Clay Carr, author of *Smart Training*, says that results from training rise or fall on whether management supports the training.
>
> In the Motorola case, managers briefed employees on what was expected from training, and after the training, debriefed employees on what they had learned.
>
>

Technology

Enacting a quality service model becomes a catalyst for change that enables leaders to lead smarter and shine in their expertise. Technology can be their best friend in this area. No longer do we need to rely on people to manage information, telephone calls, or push paper. Basic investments in technology can perform the majority of these functions.

The effective integration of technology into the customer service process enables individuals who have traditionally been locked to a desk performing administrative functions to change their focus and responsibilities toward higher quality customer interaction. This, in turn, is a huge

Technology that Supports Great Customer Service

Technology continually provides more tools to support customer service reps. Unfortunately, many companies do not take advantage of what's available, such as:

- **Call routers/schedulers.** To more intelligently utilize rep expertise and time (and schedule staffing loads). Can be combined with inbound service *and* outbound "checking in" calls to keep in touch with customers.
- **Online self-service.** (See Chapter 6 for more details.)
- **Help desks.** Intelligent databases of questions and answers allow reps to handle more issues in an increasingly effective manner.
- **Caller ID.** With records of past customer interactions immediately available, the company looks good and the reps are more efficient and effective.

opportunity to raise quality levels in service. By automating as many of these manual processes that keep individuals away from customer contact, organizations can effectively shift individual's responsibilities toward "talking to customers."

This aspect of the service model always gets positive ratings from customers and produces the "biggest bang for the buck" for the organization. How many times in today's technology-driven world do you call a company and get frustrated with voice mail? It's phenomenal!

One way to overcome these negative perceptions of your company is to shift as many people as possible toward being "live voice service agents." Smart design of this phase will be perceived by your customers as your having added a significant number of people, when in fact you just managed the technology and human resources "smarter."

> To give real service, you must add something which cannot be bought or measured with money, and that is sincerity and integrity.
> — Donald A. Adams

Trust

The final T is the essence of all successful human interactions. First, it is critical for the internal players to trust the intentions of each other. Taking care of "internal customers" is the logical first step in producing a superior service organization.

Ultimately, the goal and result is to produce external customers who trust your organization beyond the tangibles of price and products. They trust your organization beyond being satisfied.

Care About Those on the Front Lines

The frontline service providers—people—who tend to get beat up and abused and used—are the keys to success in any service organization.

What do you do to cultivate that relationship so they provide exceptional service? The . . . principle of reciprocity applies. You realize those people are in the crossfire between the demands of the customers and the operational policies of management. They are really in no-man's land, and they need to be understood and appreciated.

I've seen stewardesses on airplanes, for example, shed tears and share sad stories as they get treated poorly. Over time, some grow calloused....

In his book *My American Journey*, General Colin Powell writes disparagingly about a particular general's leadership style. "He was a tough overseer. The job got done, but by coercion, not motivation. Staff conferences turned into harangues. Inspections became inquisitions. The endless negative pressure exhausted the unit commanders and staff."

In sharp contrast, the leadership style of General Bernie Loeffke, a colleague and mentor of Colin Powell, created an esprit de corps that invigorated the troops. In Vietnam, Loeffke rewarded the top performers in his unit by allowing one man each night to sleep in his tent as he, the general, took his place on the front lines. Who would not fight for such a leader?

—Stephen Covey

They trust your organization so much that they are loyal. They become unpaid advocates and "missionaries" for your organization. This means that your quality model has superseded many tangible customer requirements and has elevated your organization to a position beyond customer satisfaction. This position is customer loyalty, the ultimate in long-term customer relationships for sustained organizational growth.

WIN! WIN! WIN!

Organizations that implement a Quality Service Model will be recognized for their excellence in all categories. Their customers will characterize them as market leaders and true pioneers in the quest for leadership of the Quality Revolution.

The win will also include the ultimate goal of all businesses: long-term, sustained growth. So, regardless of whether your organization is the well known L.L. Bean or the unknown Main Street Country Treasures, this Quality Service Model will be exactly what you need to deliver the Win! Win! Win! Here are some "wins" you can aim for, as suggested by the American Management Association.

Wins for the Customer

(1) the highest quality of products and services at the best prices
(2) greater ease of doing business
(3) continuous improvement of products and services
(4) participation in the change process

Wins for the Customer Service Rep

(1) skills enhancement tailored to the individual
(2) improved working relationships; personal pride in success
(3) more control over the work, direction, and results
(4) more opportunities for growth and new roles
(5) maximizes individual strengths and minimizes weaknesses

Wins for the Organization

(1) reduces the need for direct supervision
(2) improved quality of products and services
(3) developing solutions at all levels
(4) improved communication and commitment at all levels
(5) breaking down functional and social barriers
(6) clear vision with unified efforts
(7) improved innovation, energy, productivity, and efficiency

BURST INTO ACTION

The credit belongs to those who are actually in the arena, who strive valiantly; who know the great enthusiasms, the great devotions, and spend themselves in a worthy cause; who at best, know the triumph of high achievement; and who, at the worst, if they fail, fail while daring greatly, so that their place shall never be with those cold and timid souls who know neither the victory nor defeat.

—Theodore Roosevelt

1 Measure customer satisfaction at least once a year.

2 Identify your biggest customers and assign reps to them. (Coordinate with sales if appropriate.)

3 Create a customer advisory group.

4 Create teams responsible for service.

5 Collect and distribute stories of great service. If necessary, start with little stories of very good service.

6 Look into the ISO criterion for customer service or otherwise develop a "checklist" of what constitutes great service.

7 Create a program to build relationship trust with customers. This means contact, notes, e-mail, and so forth.

8 Create formal training goals in general, and for specific employees.

9 Identify technology that would enhance your service.

PERSONAL, PROACTIVE SERVICE THRILLS CUSTOMERS

Rick Crandall

Rick Crandall, PhD, is a consultant, writer, and speaker, specializing in talks and workshops on service, sales, and marketing. His philosophy is that business revolves around relationships with customers and the ensuing repeat business. He works largely with service providers who are uncomfortable with marketing. He has spoken for *Inc.* magazine, the American Marketing Association, Autodesk, Office Depot, and the American Society for Training and Development. Dr. Crandall has presented well over 1,000 public seminars, given many keynote presentations, and worked with organizations from large law firms to the Air Force.

He is the author or editor of six books on marketing including *1001 Ways to Market Your Services: Even If You Hate to Sell* (1998).

Dr. Crandall is the recipient of an SBA Small Business Award, and is listed in various *Who's Who*s. He edits an online marketing newsletter, *Marketing Edge*.

Rick Crandall, PhD; Agent: Select Press, PO Box 37, Corte Madera, CA 94976-0037; phone (415) 435-4461; fax (415) 435-4841; e-mail RPCrandall@aol.com.

Chapter 11

PERSONAL, PROACTIVE SERVICE THRILLS CUSTOMERS

Rick Crandall

All business is personal.
—*The Godfather*

Quite a few years ago, our office got our first postage meter. The staff was thrilled to put their stamp-licking days behind them.

One of our products was an expensive monthly newsletter that covered construction litigation. Right after we started metering our mail, one of our subscribers at a large government laboratory called to ask if we could go back to using stamps to mail out the newsletter. This seemed like an odd issue to be concerned about. Fortunately, we had the good sense to ask him why he preferred stamped mail. It turned out that he saved stamps and gave

them to a grandchild who collected them. We told the
subscriber that we'd see what we
could do.

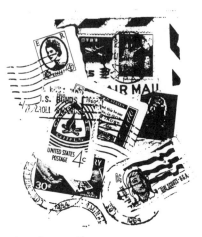

My staff was amused that a
subscriber would care about
whether his envelope was me-
tered or stamped, especially since
each month they had affixed to
his envelope the only 37¢ stamp
the post office made. (How many
specimens of the same stamp
could one man want?) However,
we realized that this was a chance to please the
customer.

As a publisher, we receive a great deal of
correspondence, much of it from overseas. So from
then on, we threw any interesting incoming stamps
into an envelope that hung on the bulletin board
in the mailing room. Besides the stamps collected
at the office, employees would bring in stamps that
had come on their personal mail. Each month, we
would send him 20–40 loose stamps. This was
superior service at a one-to-one personal level.

Unbeknownst to us, our subscriber went on
leave for almost a year. Several months into his
leave, the person who was filling in for him called.
He was bewildered as to why there were cancelled
stamps in his envelope! We explained and stopped
sending them. Even funnier is that about a year
later, the original subscriber returned to work and
called to ask where his stamps were! We resumed
sending them.

While this series of interactions was often
humorous, on the business side was that fact that
whenever his lab was considering which subscrip-
tions to renew, ours was always on the list!

PERSONAL SERVICE BUILDS RELATIONSHIPS

The earlier chapters had many suggestions on how to move ahead with a superior customer service program. The purpose of this chapter is to:

- provide you with a new perspective on building relationships with customers
- argue that the best service is both personal and proactive
- provide specific examples that you may be able to modify for your situation to create your own unique customer connections

The best service is always personal. When you do something special for someone, it stands out and you build a closer relationship. Our case of the stamps is idiosyncratic. It never happened again with any of our thousands of subscribers. And that's a big part of my point—all relationships are idiosyncratic. That's what being personal means.

Business vs. Personal

People will want different degrees of personal connection. Some will want to keep business and personal separate. It's up to you to decide for yourself and to find out where customers want to draw the line. I recommend more overlap since it's actually easier to be friends with customers than others. You will also need to be the one who takes the initiative to extend the depth of your relationships with customers.

Basic Good Service 101 and 201

Customers come to you for a product or service. You provide what they want, in a helpful way. Service 101 is to do what you say, when you say you'll do it. Sometimes you can do well at this level because other people's service is so unreliable.

To begin to thrill customers, you provide even more than they expect—Service 201. At the 101 level, you're suppose to take the initiative to learn customers' names if you interact regularly with them. At the

201 level, it's a natural step to remember more things about them and their lives. In a strictly business relationship, you might know something about their job, their boss, or their company. In a more personal relationship, you'd know about their families, hobbies, church, college, and so forth.

Advanced Service

The first idea that needs to be made explicit is that there is more to customer service than just providing good, or even great, service. You have to create a relationship.

How do you build "personal" relationships with customers, especially in large numbers? Most people want to be treated as important individuals about whom you care. Fortunately, it is relatively easy to learn how to build relationships with customers.

About 15% of Customers Don't Want Relationships

Sometimes, I as the customer will want to be anonymous. I won't want to uphold my part of a relationship, even to the extent of acknowledging that I know you. But in general, you are the one who has to do most of the work in the relationship, so it's easy for me.

You need to look for unique opportunities to respond to customers (as in our stamp example). But there are also some general ways you can use to create relationship-building opportunities. These include the following techniques:

Establish regular contact with people. In traditional marketing, you build brand awareness with regular catalogs or advertising. It reminds customers of your presence and allows them to feel a generalized relationship with you. Publicity exposure does the same thing, often with more impact.

In today's online world, an e-mail newsletter is ideal for building awareness while keeping in touch in a more personal way. It's informal but can provide useful information. You can maintain regular contact at almost no cost to you.

The newsletter material must be interesting to the recipient, not self-serving for you. Sending out a printed newsletter, or mailing or faxing jokes or industry information, are similar approaches. I read a lot, so clipping articles of interest to customers is easy for me. Now I can also forward online articles.

> People like to be recognized because they see themselves as important and worthwhile. A business that acknowledges this importance is a business that maintains customer esteem.
> —Schneider and Bowen, *Winning the Marketing Game*

Find out how each customer wants to be treated. Sometimes this is subtle personality information that may be difficult to understand. But often it's just a matter of asking them or their staff, or observing their responses. Some will like more schmoozing, jokes, or industry gossip. Others will be all business.

Ask questions and make notes. In order to find similar interests, and the style your customers prefer, you need to listen a lot more than you talk. For instance, their birthdays, favorite hobbies, and past jobs are basic information to have.

Find out what their passions are in life. This gives you a chance to build rapport, find appropriate presents, and always have something to talk about.

Give it time. "Business expert" Woody Allen said something like 90% of success is just showing up. It's surprisingly true. Staying around and in contact will do a lot for you. Research shows that we like new "things" more the more frequently we see them. It works for people, too. Plus you have more time to build rapport and learn about their situations. This allows you to provide personal service more easily.

REACTIVE VS. PROACTIVE

If you look at the examples of ways to build relationships with customers, I think you will see that many involve your being *proactive*. Personalized service that builds relationships will usually involve your taking the initiative.

Average customer service is *reactive*. Customers come to you and you respond. Even traditional ideas for great service are reactive. Customers come to you and you provide what they want plus something extra. You are taking some initiative, but only in response to the customer's wishes.

Reactive Service

Look at the chances you have to provide service or build relationships that are reactive:

1. when they purchase
2. when they contact you about possibly purchasing
3. when you thank them for a referral
4. when they come to you with a problem
5. when you see them accidently on the street or at a business meeting

You can see that there aren't very many reactive opportunities to show your great service, and they are not always under your control.

Proactive Service

Now look at your chances to provide more personal service and build relationships that are proactive:

1. when something new comes out in their area of interest you notify them
2. your regularly scheduled newsletter or online letter (ezine)
3. their anniversary of doing business with you, or other holidays or milestones
4. acknowledging their kids' birthdays, that their team won, clippings about their personal interests

> It seems fair to conclude from research that 70% of customers who defected did so because they didn't like the human side of doing business with the previous service provider.
> —Tom Peters

5. their national industry week, or conventions
6. random calls to say hello, how's it going?
7. inviting them to a seminar on a business topic
8. customer satisfaction surveys
9. inviting them to a customer advisory panel or focus group
10. plant tours, open houses
11. giving them tickets to an event
12. when you give others a referral to them for their business

You can see that there are a lot more opportunities for your service and relationship to stand out when you are proactive. And, by definition, they're under your control.

Proactivity is more personal. Proactivity has another advantage. Many of these proactive service suggestions also involve personal, rather than business, interactions. Since the majority of the business contacts are reactive, they will have less impact. In other words, customers are less impressed when you are simply reacting to their business needs. When you take initiative on a more personal basis, you gain the additional impact of both "personalness" and proactivity.

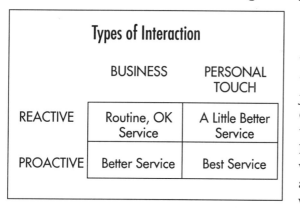

Types of Interaction		
	BUSINESS	PERSONAL TOUCH
REACTIVE	Routine, OK Service	A Little Better Service
PROACTIVE	Better Service	Best Service

Benefits When You Take Initiative. You have several advantages when you take the initiative:

- extra opportunities to make a good impression
- you can control the scheduling

- more perceived sincerity—when you contact customers and aren't trying to sell them something, your interest seems more sincere

When you react to my contact, I may be pleased by good service, but you're really just doing your job. When you take the initiative to do something for me, I'm more likely to be impressed or feel special.

The Joy of Service

In many ways, taking the initiative to thrill customers and build personal relationships is easy. It makes your job fun. Customer service is a chance for person-to-person interaction. And if your customers are used to the mediocre service most of us get most of the time, they'll appreciate you all the more.

Proactive Internal Service

Proactivity is also important for internal customer service. If someone helps you only when asked, it's much less appreciated than when they volunteer. Or when management responds to a workers' request, it's good. But when management offers something without being asked, it's better.

CONCRETE EXAMPLES

My classification of service and relationship building into reactive and proactive is a model to help make an important distinction. It should give you some ideas you can start to apply. The simplest one is to begin to take more initiative in providing service to your customers.

In order to "prime the pump" for you, what follows are a number of examples of better, or great, service. They don't all fall neatly into simple reactive vs. proactive or business vs. personal categories, but you'll find some great ways to thrill customers. See how many you can adapt to your situation.

Glorify the Client

To show their devotion to their clients, an advertising agency set up a "war room" for each major client's work. Each war room was painted the client's colors, and the client's account strategy material was posted on the walls. A dedicated room pulls together research material and allows focused meetings. It also reminds employees who's the boss (the client!) and the clients love having space dedicated to them.

Offer Extras

The Fingerhut catalog company uses complicated mathematical models to measure the lifetime value of customers. The models are proprietary, so you'll have to develop your own. But what it means for customers is a lesson anyone can apply. When their best potential customers order by mail, Fingerhut calls to confirm their orders and tells them when they will arrive. They then offer to let you "opt-in" to receive special offers. And they offer personalized services such as entering the birthdays of family members and receiving reminders and custom offers to make present-giving easy.

Stay with the Customer

A common frustration for customers who phone is to be forwarded around a company in search of the "right" office. The first person you talk to should take care of it. If they can't, they shouldn't just pass you off into phone limbo. At the Apple tech support line, a problem was diagnosed. Arrangements needed to be made for repair. Instead of simply transferring the customer to appointments, the service rep

Dealing with Jerks

When customers are jerks—and they can be—the psychological strategy of detachment can be useful. It's surprising what a difference this can make in your state of mind. Some ways to do this are:
- Pretend you're observing the situation from "outside" yourself.
- Pretend you're a reporter or author looking for examples of terrible customer behavior. Make mental notes and write it down afterward.
- Better yet, get your company to offer a small prize for the worst customer horror story (as mentioned in Chapter 9). Thinking that this customer could help you win gives you a new perspective!

made the phone transfer and stayed on the line until the connection was made. Similarly, when you ask where something is when you're shopping at Safeway, clerks are trained to offer to take you to the item, or just to automatically walk you there.

Database Customization

"Neural nets" and other "smart" databases can learn your customers' habits and present material to them in the order that is likely to be relevant to them. For example, some Internet search engines, such as Magellan and Metacrawler, rank what they find in the order they think it best matches your request. This approach is ideal for online catalogs. For instance, RS Components in the United Kingdom offers more than 100,000 industrial items. On their Web site, a different, customized catalog is presented for each customer based on their buying and search behaviors. Every interaction "teaches" the catalog to do a better job for each customer.

Another example is the technology that Amazon.com and others use to suggest items you might like based on your similarity to other buyers. For example, if you buy the underground classic movie, *The Princess Bride*, the software can tell you what movies other people who bought this movie have also bought: You are provided with suggestions customized for you.

> Raving fans are made by meeting expectations plus 1% more. That may not seem like much, but 1% repeated adds up to a lot.
> —Ken Blanchard ("The One Minute Manager")

Extra Follow-Up

Research shows that a professional appointment with a doctor plus a follow-up call to see how you're doing is seen by the patient as much better service than the same service without the call. Hospitals can be particularly aggravating with their delays and emphasis on form-filling and insurance more than service.

At the small Tahoe Forest Hospital, when the patient came in with a history of intestinal block-

A Timeless Lesson

by Tom Peters

The idea of . . . connections . . . is to forge close, lasting intimate relationships . . . with customers, even masses of customers, one at a time . . . Take the little case of M. H. N. Tattersall, an Australian physician. *The Wall Street Journal* describes an experiment he conducted on office procedures. After the visit of 48 patients, the doctor randomly split them into two categories. Half got follow-up letters, half didn't. Thirteen of the 24 who got letters later said they were "completely satisfied," the highest possible rating. Only four of the 24 nonrecipients made the same assessment. Think about that: A mere letter increased the number of fully satisfied customers by a factor of more than three.

What is a visit to a doctor? It's a complex event. Dr. Tattersall . . . brings years of scientific training and experience to bear on a diagnosis. Yet this one time twist, a follow-up letter, can completely change the patient's perception of the service rendered. Look at it another way. A doctor's consultation plus a letter is an entirely different service/product from a consultation without a letter . . .

I am suggesting that the technical part of "your act" is far from the whole story and that the worth of the nontechnical elements is often badly underestimated, or not even considered.

age and great pain, she was taken to a bed *before* the forms were handled, even though her husband was there to fill them out. Staff and nurses showed pride in their hospital which convinced them to let an operation go ahead in this "small time" setting. Doctors and nurses showed respect. Even the emergency room nurse checked in every day to see how recuperation was going. And the doctor called *three times* after she went home to see how she was doing.

Handling Problems

Statistics suggest that customers are actually more loyal to you after they've had a problem and you've taken care of it than if they'd never had a problem at all. The rumor is that one computer company took this to its logical conclusion—they built a bug into their own system on purpose! Then when customers called because things didn't work and they handled it brilliantly, customers would be impressed and more loyal! Of course, no one admits to this kind of deliberate sabotage.

Waiting at home for utility connections is a pain. When the GTE phone company missed an appointment, the customer called the next day to complain. GTE apologized for their mistake, put a rush on the appointment, showed up within an hour, and gave the customer a $100 credit on her phone bill. She reported, "It was hard to believe I was dealing with the phone company," and felt positive about a negative situation.

> The Internet is filled with innovations that allow companies to build learning relationships with customers.
>
> —Don Peppers

Locking Customers In with Extras

Some service starts as reactive and then goes beyond expectations to be proactive. Sometimes you use hidden technology customers aren't even aware of. In these cases, you have a competitive edge when they can't find the same level of service elsewhere.

The authors of the important books, *The One to One Future* and *Enterprise One to One* (Don Peppers and Martha Rogers), have a favorite tactic in this regard. By investing in learning about your customers' requirements, the customers have also invested time in you. If you do a good job, customers will not want to switch and pay the cost of "retraining" your competitors.

Vodac is a South African mobile phone company. They give subscribers the ability to create 100-number personal phone directories that can be dialed automatically. Customer can also send the same message to multiple numbers, including predesignated groups (such as bridge club members). Of course, if you leave, you lose your phone directory. Vodak also prepares your bill any way you like it,

Serving the Needs of Waiting People

A big car wash in Chicago installed rabbit-petting pens, an aquarium, a sun deck, and a game table for kids. They also offer free popcorn.

The Coin Laundry Association says 90% of their members now provide ancillary activities.

Some restaurants offer pagers to guests so they can go for a walk or window shop while waiting for a table.

A writer in *Newsweek* suggests that retail shops provide waiting areas. He says he just wants a chair to sit in while his wife shops. "How about a companion support center?" he asked. "Shoppers would be motivated knowing their companions were relaxing in a chair, not brooding or nursing anger. They would have time to buy more."

The Power of the Personal Touch

A nursing home manager noticed that almost all of the letters praising the facility came from the families of patients served by one particular nurse. This nurse always took the time to greet each family member by name and tell them how their loved one had done since their last visit.

Management used the nurse's behavior as a model for a training program, and this nursing home had a waiting list while others had unused capacity.

—Rick Crandall,
1001 Ways to
Market Your
Services: Even If
You Hate to Sell

including on spreadsheets that interface with your computer system. And the information is available online, which cuts service inquiries to Vodac by 20%.

Little Things Mean a Lot

Cyber-cards.com offered a special advertising discount to members of one online list. They provided very good service by producing the ads fast (typical "Internet time") with a few extra bells and whistles. Then they duplicated the ads free on a sister Web site for extra exposure. This bonus created customer loyalty and more word-of-mouth advertising. Such extras are easy to provide in cyberspace where the "space" is free. But almost any business can offer extras with real perceived value that cost them next to nothing.

Building in a Personal Connection

Roberts Express has grown by customizing its delivery abilities and personalizing its service. Customers are assigned based on region in order to allow reps to get to know them. And for individual shipments, one rep follows it through the whole process. This means that special shipping preferences are not only noted, but are "top of the mind" for reps. Automatic phone routing of calls and special connections to trucks on the road make the process practical. But from the customer's point of view, they are simply getting personal—and better—service.

High Tech, High Touch

The goal of high technology should be to serve us, not vice versa. A business traveler is on the road meeting clients. His wife is in a meeting and unavailable. His son, who is backpacking in Europe, has broken a tooth and is in too much pain to travel. He reaches his father by phone in New York. The father calls Thomas Cook. Through technology, the rep is able to immediately find out about the family's health insurance. She then finds an English-speaking dentist within a few miles of the son, wires cash to the son's youth hostel, and rearranges his travel plans. Then she calls the wife in San Francisco with a report and tells her the son is fine. That's the kind of service most of us don't receive even once in a lifetime!

Act as a True Consultant

When growing firms want to go public, they are advised to get a "Big 6" (now Big 4) audit. Many small accounting firms that have helped the clients grow fight this trend, arguing correctly that they are better able to do the audit. However, the public marketplace wants a Big 4 audit anyway. One small accounting firm referred their client to a Big 4 firm early, so the client would have an "acceptable" financial history and the Big 4 firm would have more time to get to know the client. By making the referral themselves, they acted as a consultant in the client's best interest. And they had time to help the client select

Santa Claus Service

In most of my books, I mention an example I've developed from Kris Kringle in the classic movie, *Miracle on 34th Street.* When Kris started sending shoppers to other stores because it best served their needs, he was taking initiative in a surprising way. These referrals clearly demonstrated that he cared more about customers' personal satisfaction than he did about Macy's making the sale. That's great service and relationship building. It makes for very loyal customers when you put their interests clearly above yours. And it makes you a valued resource rather than a "vendor."

Giving your cusotmers what they want is one thing. Giving them what they want before they know they want it is what superior performance is all about.

—The Forum Corporation

the right firm. Even though they gave up some work before they needed to, they strengthened their position to do the "routine" work forever.

Personalizing a Commodity

N.V. Nutsbedrijf Westland is a natural gas distributor in Holland. Many of their customers are flower growers using heated greenhouses. Rather than just selling them fuel, Westland will install computers that help maintain the proper CO_2 output, humidity, light, and other factors, as well as temperature at optimum efficiency. By offering them more than the commodity, customers would have to give up a system that helps their businesses in order to switch.

Be Dramatic: Create a Performance

Where's the last place you expect to get good service? How about on a commuter train into New York City. Meet urban legend Travis Ford. First, he is personal and friendly, remembering passengers and their interests. More dramatically, he gives a presentation on the weather, the five-day forecast, baseball matchups and the television schedules for the games. Passengers applaud and warm up to each other, making the whole trip a pleasure. Unfortunately, the train company has not acknowledged this superior service provider or used him as a role model for others.

Varian Associates makes semiconductor equipment. They've used a video helmet to link customers with support offices. The helmet can send a video of a problem and engineers can reply to the helmet with audio, video, photos, and even drawings to solve the problem. It's almost as good as a virtual reality game for clients. And it's so novel that it makes a big impression.

CONCLUSION

The message of this book is simple: Great service makes a big difference—for your customers, employees, and profits. Service today is often lacking, especially in contrast to the stories of legendary service, like those about Nordstrom, that we have all heard. In the future, extraordinary service will be even more expected. If you're going to excel, you must make a commitment to great service.

The message of this chapter is also simple. Customer service will be limited when you rely on being reactive and "business-like." To be great, you need to be proactive and personal. This gives you a number of advantages, not least of which is surprising customers and being able to control how you build the relationship with them.

This book has provided lots of examples of how to build a great customer service program. The most important thing you can do now is to get started. Good luck!

EXPLODE INTO ACTION

The best time to plant a tree was 20 years ago. The next best time is today.

—Ancient Chinese saying

1   Create a database to record information about your customers. Look especially for things they care about professionally or personally.

2   Maintain regular contact with customers by sending out an online newsletter that benefits them.

3   Talk to your best customers and find out how they want to be treated. Set up a mechanism to treat each one, or group, differently.

4 Determine how good your reactive service is. Specify when you have the opportunity to react to customers. Write down the kinds of things you can do to provide extras to customers or make up for mistakes.

5 Create a list of the proactive things you could do to build your relationships with customers.

6 Pick at least three examples of superior service from the chapter that you can adapt to your situation.

7 Create your own list of super service examples. Post or circulate them.

8 What can you do that will create a performance or entertain your customers? How about at a trade show? How about a skit for your internal customers, spoofing management and making the point about needed service levels?

9 Set up a recognition and reward program to encourage all of the above. (See Chapter 3.)

10 Get started this week on something.

NOTE: Some of the examples in this chapter are adapted from the *Inside 1 to 1* newsletter by Peppers and Rogers.

INDEX